ANATOMY
OF A
PONZI

SCAMS PAST AND PRESENT

COLLEEN CROSS

ANATOMY OF A PONZI
Schemes Past and Present

Colleen Tompkins writing as Colleen Cross
Copyright © 2013 by Colleen Cross, Colleen Tompkins

ISBN: 978-0-9878835-3-7 Paperback
ISBN: 978-0-9878835-4-4 Ebook

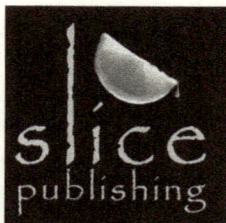

slice
publishing

Published by Slice Publishing
Cover art: Streetlight Graphics
Author Photo: Trevor Hallam
For information contact Colleen Cross: http://www.ColleenCross.com

CHAPTER 1

THE MAKINGS OF A PONZI SCHEME

C HARLES PONZI WASN'T THE FIRST Ponzi schemer, though he did lend his catchy name to this age-old fraud. Before Ponzi became a household word, this time-tested swindle went by other names. Shady characters have always practiced the art of deception to enrich themselves at the expense of others.

Since Ponzi's scam in 1920, more than one hundred massive Ponzi schemes have been uncovered in the United States alone. That equals more than one per year, counting only the ones where the perpetrators were caught. Those discovered represent the tip of an iceberg in a sea of undetected frauds. Ponzi schemes are now more common than ever and on a financial scale that dwarfs Ponzi's $20-million scam.

More than a few large Ponzi schemes are in play right now, operating under the radar and duping ordinary people like you and me. Many have operated unhindered for decades. When the next big one is finally exposed, it will dwarf Bernard Madoff's massive $65-billion fraud of the century. The Ponzi schemes in this book appear complicated at first blush, but they are not. The illusion of complexity is an integral part of the fraud itself. Distill a Ponzi down to its essential ingredients and you will see how surprisingly simple it is to spot one.

Ponzi 101

A Ponzi scheme is a fraudulent investment scheme promising unusually high returns, often over a short period of time. The get-rich-quick promise is so attractive that even conservative investors find it impossible to pass up. Fantastic returns are the hallmark of a Ponzi scheme.

In reality, the profits investors are paid are just a return of their original investment, or the capital of later investors. The scam works as long as new money keeps flowing in. That money can be from new investors, but an integral part of most Ponzi schemes is convincing existing investors to re-invest their proceeds and ideally contribute even more.

Many do, since the Ponzi scheme promises much higher returns than an investor can find anywhere else. This is how otherwise astute investors succumb to greed and put all (or most of) their funds into one investment. More often than not, they lose their life's savings. Usually the investment is described in vague terms or in jargon too complicated for the average person to fully understand. This is done on purpose. Complexity obfuscates the painful truth: there is no underlying investment.

Charles Ponzi and the other swindlers portrayed in this book were exceptionally talented at obtaining new money from investors (or individuals). They were superb promoters and sealed the deal with lucrative payments, at least at first. Investors saw fantastic returns from their initial investments, far exceeding what they could earn elsewhere. They let their greed sway them into investing more and more money into the scheme.

Before a fraudster can separate you from your money, he or she must build your confidence. A common selling technique of Ponzi schemes is the lure of a practically risk-free investment that pays off over a very short period. Many Ponzi victims are skeptical until they receive the first payment or two of the promised returns. That's usually enough to convince them of the investment's legitimacy. They then reinvest the proceeds and often increase the size of their investment. In order for the schemes to work, there is almost always initial "success" for the investor. The early payout is the carrot. From that point on, it's much easier to dupe the investor into contributing more money.

Think it couldn't happen to you? Bernie Madoff's hedge fund investors never expected to be swindled either. Madoff defrauded seasoned investment professionals, astute managers of family trusts and even other hedge funds, the so-called "feeder funds" that invested their money into the Madoff fund. Despite their financial sophistication, these experts were captivated by the promise of lucrative returns.

Many charitable organizations were duped into investing with Madoff, including Steven Spielberg's Wunderkinder Foundation. Madoff's victims list reads like a who's who of celebrities. Kevin Bacon, Kyra Sedgwick, Larry King, and even the late John Denver's estate all had a stake in his scheme. Former New York state attorney general Eliot Spitzer's family firm was also defrauded.

In the chapters that follow, we will study Madoff's Ponzi scheme and others. Once you know how to spot a Ponzi scheme, you can avoid becoming a victim.

A Ponzi Page from the Middle Ages

Ponzi schemes have occurred in one form or another since bartering began, becoming more sophisticated as the concepts of currency and investing evolved. The age-old con plays out repeatedly on unsuspecting investors today.

You have probably heard the phrase "rob Peter to pay Paul." Simply put, the phrase means to take money from one person only to pay a debt owed to another. This phrase has been in use as far back as 1450, and it likely referred to the same ruse. Here is the original phrase from around 1450 when it appeared in *Jacob's well: an English Treatise on the cleansing of man's conscience*:

*"To robbe Petyr & geve it Poule, it were
non almesse but gret synne."*

While today (and today's English) differs from 1450 England, the phrase describes exactly what a Ponzi scheme does. It pays returns to earlier investors with the money from later contributors. The schemer gives you money he claims is your investment profits. And what profits they are—multiples of the best return you could achieve anywhere else.

The investment earnings are a fabrication, a ploy to build trust and convince you to part with even more of your money. As your confidence builds, the fraudster hopes you will increase your investment and convince others to invest too. He uses illusion and psychological tricks to cheat you out of your own money in this old-fashioned confidence game.

The con was well known in nineteenth-century England. It even featured prominently in a few Charles Dickens books. In *Martin Chuzzlewitt*, The Anglo-Bengalee Disinterested Loan and Life Assurance Company uses proceeds from newer policyholders to pay off earlier ones. In *Little Dorrit*, Mr.Merdle enticed investors with fantastic returns on deposits, when in reality he used their money to hide his misappropriation of earlier depositors' money. Dickens' upbringing piqued his interest in these financial schemes.

Dickens' father spent money lavishly and lived far beyond his means. When John Dickens was unable to pay his £40 (£3,018 in 2013) debt to a baker in 1824, the father of eight was imprisoned in Marshalsea

Debtor's prison in Southwark (now within London city limits). Charles was just twelve, but had to leave school for a job at Warren's blacking factory, where he worked 10 hours a day for 6 shillings a week.

At that time, all prisons were privately run for profit, and charged their captives "prison fees" which further decreased their ability to repay debts. As the fees compounded, additional time was added onto an inmate's sentence. Some prison stays extended to decades, even though most debts amounted to less than £20. Many inmates even starved to death, as they were required to provide their own food and clothing.

Dickens resented the loss of his childhood freedom, and financial themes abound throughout his works. Many of his stories portray working-class people taken advantage of by financial scam artists. John Dickens was not a Ponzi schemer, but Charles seemed to have been intrigued by the financial crimes he built into his stories. Perhaps he met a few real-life Ponzi schemers during his frequent visits to the prison.

Today we have laws and regulations to protect us. We are better informed and more sophisticated investors when compared to the easy prey of earlier times. Yet regardless of safeguards, Ponzi schemes are more common than ever.

Most fraud is still uncovered by chance. Despite technology, regulations, and access to more information than ever, fraud is rarely uncovered by investors or regulators. Instead, an external event is often the catalyst, such as the 2008 financial crisis. As markets plunged and liquidity dried up, investors redeemed their investments. Many Ponzi schemes, including the Madoff one, collapsed when they couldn't keep up with the redemptions. Suddenly there was no new investor money to pay off the earlier investors.

Present-Day—Ponzi Top Ten

The top ten Ponzi schemes (by financial losses) of all time all occurred since 1990. Half of these were exposed during the 2008 financial crisis.

Rank	Fraudster	Date Exposed	Scam	Amount (USD)
1	Bernard Madoff	2008	Bernard L. Madoff Investment Securities LLC (USA)	65 billion
2	Sergey Mavrodi	1990	MMM, reseller (Russia)	10 billion
3	Allen Stanford	2009	Stanford International Bank (Antigua)	7 billion
4	Tom Petters	2008	Petters Group Worldwide, reseller (USA)	3.7 billion
5	Scott Rothstein	2009	Structured Settlements (USA)	1.4 billion
6	Damara Bertges	1994	European Kings Club (Germany, Switzerland)	1.1 billion
7	Ioan Stoica	1994	Caritas Company (Romania)	1 billion
8	Nevin Shapiro	2009	Grocery diverting, reseller (USA)	900 million
9	Marc Dreier	2008	Dreier LLP – forged promissory notes (USA)	750 million
10	Paul Burks	2012	ZeekRewards (USA)	600 million

CHAPTER 2

PORTRAIT OF A FRAUDSTER

C ON ARTISTS COME FROM ALL walks of life. Some grew up poor, bent on achieving wealth at any cost. Others, like Marc Dreier, came from affluent families and enjoyed every advantage. Bernard Madoff rose from a modest background, but he was already a millionaire by the time he started his Ponzi scheme.

What drives people to jeopardize their reputations and livelihoods? Why do they risk branding as a criminal, and potentially conviction to serve jail time? Surprisingly, money is often not the core motivator behind the crime, although it may have provided the initial attraction. Often the driving force is ego, or a need to feel important.

Regardless of how they start, most fraudsters seek the adulation that comes with prestige and power. They often enjoy the thrill of deceit, knowing they can manipulate and cheat anyone out of anything. Power and recognition fuel their egos, and money is simply the vehicle to get there.

Financial Psychopaths

While circumstances might differ, most Ponzi

schemers share some common personality traits. Many are sociopaths or psychopaths. They almost have to be, to carry out their crimes without conscience. How else could they act with the full knowledge of the financial ruin they bring upon their unsuspecting victims? They connive and steal from the elderly or unsophisticated without an ounce of guilt or remorse, and could not care less about the trail of destruction they leave. They are only concerned with their own needs.

Many say they intended to pay the money back. They claim a temporary setback made them "borrow" the money. It is an all-too convenient excuse. When you delve into the details you find that in most cases, they have perpetuated their frauds for years, even decades.

Most fraudsters are so confident they won't get caught that they often steal from their own family members or friends. Their grandiose sense of self-worth, arrogance and feeling of superiority over others is truly staggering.

The only good thing about their pretentious attitude is that it often results in their downfall. Arrogance blinds them to the flaws in their schemes, and is often why they are eventually exposed.

Of course, not all Ponzi schemers are psychopaths, nor is every psychopath hatching a Ponzi scheme. However, as we study the personalities behind the biggest Ponzi schemes in history, you will notice some striking similarities. Research into the minds of Ponzi schemers has shown a truly astonishing number of them exhibit psychopathic traits.

Portrait of a Fraudster

Dr. Robert D. Hare[1], the developer of the Hare Psychology Checklist (PCL-R), includes the following as key characteristics of a psychopath:

1. Glib and Superficial Charm—the tendency to be smooth, engaging, charming, slick, and verbally facile. They are not in the least shy, self-conscious, or afraid to say anything. Psychopaths never get tongue-tied.

2. Grandiose Self-Worth—a grossly inflated view of one's abilities and self-worth, self-assured, opinionated, cocky, a braggart. They are arrogant people who believe they are superior human beings.

3. Need for Stimulation or Proneness to Boredom— an excessive need for novel, thrilling, and exciting stimulation; taking chances and doing things that are risky. Psychopaths rarely carry tasks through to completion because they are easily bored. Many fail to work at the same job for any length of time, for example, or to finish tasks that they consider dull or routine.

4. Pathological Lying—can be moderate or high; in moderate form, psychopaths will be shrewd, crafty, cunning, sly, and clever; in extreme form, they will be deceptive, deceitful, underhanded, unscrupulous, manipulative, and dishonest.

1   The Hare Psychopathy Checklist-Revised by Robert D. Hare, 1991. Multi-Health Systems, 908 Niagara Falls Blvd, North Tonawanda, New York, USA, 14120-2060

5. Conning and Manipulativeness—the use of deceit and deception to cheat, con, or defraud others for personal gain; distinguished from Item #4 in the degree to which exploitation and callous ruthlessness is present, as reflected in a lack of concern for the feelings and suffering of one's victims.

6. Lack of Remorse or Guilt—a lack of feelings or concern for the losses, pain, and suffering of victims; a tendency to be unconcerned, dispassionate and coldhearted.

7. Shallow Affect—emotional poverty or a limited range or depth of feelings; interpersonal coldness in spite of signs of open gregariousness.

8. Callousness and Lack of Empathy—a lack of feelings toward people in general; cold, contemptuous, inconsiderate, and tactless.

9. Parasitic Lifestyle—an intentional, manipulative, selfish, and exploitative financial dependence on others as reflected in a lack of motivation, low self-discipline, and inability to begin or complete responsibilities.

10. Poor Behavioral Controls—expressions of irritability, annoyance, impatience, threats, aggression, and verbal abuse; inadequate control of anger and temper; acting hastily.

This is only a portion of Hare's PCL-R checklist, but

you get the picture. All of the above are perfect traits for a Ponzi schemer. Even qualified clinicians find it difficult to confirm a psychopath diagnosis. Ticking the boxes is not all that is involved in identifying a psychopath. However, it raises a fundamental question. Why would we ever trust our money to people with these characteristics?

Scott Rothstein, disbarred Florida lawyer and perpetrator of a $1.4 billion Ponzi scheme, certainly displayed most of the characteristics. His extravagant purchases included his million-dollar watch collection, exotic cars, and luxury real estate. But he didn't stop there. His freewheeling spending also included over-the-top contributions to political parties to curry favor, and he also made charitable donations to fuel his need for name recognition and publicity. Even after he was caught red-handed and admitted guilt, he briefly escaped to Morocco. He had secretly squirreled away money there, after having the presence of mind to first confirm the absence of an extradition treaty.

Bernie Madoff showed no remorse after committing the largest Ponzi fraud in history. The former NASDAQ chairman was already a billionaire, so he didn't need the money. He was fabulously wealthy, moved in exclusive circles, and was so well-regarded that even seasoned hedge fund managers begged to invest their money with him. Madoff also had all the trappings of wealth: a yacht in the French Riviera, a couple of jets at his disposal, and just like Rothstein, an expensive watch collection.

More aloof than Rothstein, Madoff nevertheless

ingratiated himself with important people, like Wall Street regulators. Such networking further cultivated his image as a Wall Street elder statesman. Like Rothstein, he had a grandiose sense of ego and superiority, and a complete lack of empathy for his victims. Even after admitting his guilt, he seemed more concerned about his reputation than the lives he had ruined. A fraudster's view of the world always focuses on the fraudster, not you.

Can Madoff, Rothstein, and other fraudsters be considered psychopaths? Only their psychologists know for sure. Many never started out with the express intention to defraud others. Given the right motivations and circumstances, almost anyone can commit fraud. It has less to do with upbringing, social status, or ambition than you might think. As we have already seen, money is often a secondary factor.

Aside from a fraudster's psyche, there are some outward signs you can look for. Many con artists are overly concerned about image. They may boast about their connections or need to feel important. Many will donate large sums of other people's money to charity, for the express purpose of getting a hospital wing or a school named after them.

They often own expensive cars, yachts and homes, or flashy jewelry. Only the best is good enough for them in terms of travel, clothes and the other trappings of wealth. Image is paramount. They want to appear ultra-rich and successful, perhaps as further proof that you should invest with them.

Some like to rub shoulders with elite athletes, celebrities, and politicians. Nevin Shapiro spent millions as a football booster, just so he could hang out with University of Miami basketball players and NBA stars. Once he faced jail time for his Ponzi scheme, he lashed out at the University of Miami sports program and accused athletes of violating the rules by accepting his gifts. If he was going down, he decided to take others with him, even those not connected to his Ponzi scheme. His ego demanded it.

To Catch a Thief

Aside from psychology, people reveal their characters most clearly by their everyday actions. Look at the person behind the investment, and spend a few minutes on a background check. Much of the information below can be found online, in public records or media reports.

While a background check does not indicate whether this person is running a Ponzi scheme, it will reveal plenty about the integrity and character of the person promoting the investment.

Someone exhibiting some or all of the following traits may not have much of a conscience. At best, they are likely dishonest in at least some personal or business dealings. Why assume they will be honest or have integrity in their business dealings with you?

1. Speeding tickets or motor vehicle infractions
    Almost everyone gets speeding tickets from time to time. But people repeatedly ticketed show a blatant disregard for laws and regulations. These types of people often decide the rules apply to other people and

not to them. Very often, they do not pay the fines, either. Their sidestepping of rules can apply in other areas too, like securities regulations. Avoid investing with someone who skirts the law.

2. Extramarital affairs

Anyone engaged in deception of any kind shows tendencies toward self-gratification and an alarming lack of ethics and morals.

3. Professional or business disputes

Most fraudsters have a prior history of business disputes, litigation, and even prior fraud charges. Several or more former business associates may also refuse to engage in business deals with the person, or even to have contact with them. They may be unwilling to say why, since the fraudster often uses offense as a defense. He may threaten litigation. This sort of thing is not hard to uncover with all the information available online today.

4. Disciplined or investigated by regulatory bodies in the past

Disciplinary action is usually preceded by repeated warnings. Most people are disciplined only after all else fails.

5. Criminal past

It is surprising how many people have a

history of repeated criminal convictions for fraud, yet they are able to repeat similar or even identical crimes on unsuspecting victims.

The Fraud Triangle

While personality and psychology play a major role in a fraudster's actions, there are other equally important considerations. Donald R. Cressey was a noted criminologist, sociologist, and penologist, and was widely considered a pioneer in the study of white-collar crime. In the 1950s, he interviewed more than a hundred inmates convicted of embezzlement to understand their behavior and motivations. He identified three common traits, which when present *together* could lead to fraudulent behavior. This combination is commonly referred to as *Cressey's Fraud Triangle:*

1. Financial problems defined as non-sharable as well as the opportunity to violate trust

2. Knowledge of the workings of the specific enterprise

3. Rationalization of the act

Cressey's fraud triangle related more to embezzling employees, but the principles apply to any situation where the opportunity for fraud is present. With the right access and knowledge, all that is missing is rationalization, or an excuse. Some fraudsters don't expressly plan to start a Ponzi scheme. After a few bad investments or cash flow problems, they realize they are unable to escape the financial mess they have created. Rather than confess their mistakes, they hide their losses and rationalize their deception by telling themselves they are temporarily borrowing the funds. When things get better, they will repay the money and no one will be the wiser. Of course, repayment never happens, often because it isn't possible. Once they are no longer able to attract new investor money to pay off earlier investors, they are exposed.

Regardless of how the fraud and deception began, these fraudsters are hardly trustworthy characters. Further, their claims that their scheme started out legitimately might be self-serving. When the scheme is eventually unwound, the fraud inception date becomes critically important, since it determines the division of any remaining funds amongst the victims. Investor returns paid prior to the fraud start date are considered legitimate and belong to the investors receiving them. However, profits received after the fraud starts do not belong to recipients, since they were paid from the funds of earlier investors.

Net winners under the scheme must surrender their so-called "earnings". Recovered monies are re-apportioned amongst the net winners and net losers. This ensures everyone shares in the loss, since the earnings were not real in the first place. It is similar to confiscating stolen goods from those who purchased them. The stolen items get returned to the rightful owners, and the unwitting buyer is left out of pocket.

Bernard Madoff claimed that his Ponzi scheme

started from a legitimate investment fund. That may be, except he has a vested interest in choosing a later start date for the fraud. The later date benefits his earlier investors (who also happened to be family and former friends).

Any claim of a Ponzi being unintentional should be taken with a grain of salt. The difference between a premeditated and an unintentional Ponzi schemer is simply degree of rationalization. Somewhere along the timeline they are all pre-meditated, since they are committed with the express intention of stealing from others.

The Accountant's Handbook of Fraud and Commercial Crime also summarizes the essential ingredients for a fraud in the *GONE* theory:

Greed

Opportunity

Need

Expectation (of not being caught)

While greed drives the desire for money and riches, an opportunity must be present. This serves as a trigger for the person to put his wants into action. Most people with a conscience will still not commit fraud, since the risk of exposure, reputational damage, and imprisonment far outweigh any potential reward.

A greater need must drive an individual to crime, whether it be ego, a drug addiction, or a need to cover up previous investment losses. Ego is the overwhelming core need for most Ponzi schemers. Though they need to cover up financial losses, these losses only occur once their schemes are underway. Very few Ponzi schemers are substance abusers, simply because they are too busy doctoring client statements and financial records.

The last barrier to committing fraud—fear of being caught—is removed if the perpetrator believes he can conceal the fraud. Most fraudsters studied in this book restricted financial record access to only themselves or a trusted few. They also kept their offices locked and were much more "hands-on" than typical executives.

Given the right circumstances, anyone can hatch a Ponzi scheme.

CHAPTER 3

CHARLES PONZI—NOT THE FIRST, OR THE LAST

Ponzi Particulars	Charles Ponzi
Theme	The Securities Exchange Company, international postal reply coupons
Fraud	$20 million ($225 million in today's dollars)
Promised return	100% in 90 days
Investors defrauded	Thousands (exact number unknown)
Date discovered	1920s
Where	Boston, Massachusetts
Prison sentence	12 years

Boston, Massachusetts—1918

CHARLES PONZI GLANCED AROUND HIS 5th-floor office in the grimy Niles Building on School Street. His Boston business address could not hide the fact that he was a complete and utter failure. His current business venture had not panned out, the latest in a string of failures. He had no rent money, and his office furniture was about to be repossessed. Worst of all, he had run out of lies to tell his mother back in Parma, Italy.

His circumstances were not what he had envisioned when he had disembarked from the SS Vancouver in Boston Harbor in 1903 with a few dollars in his pocket and a big dream. Here he was, fifteen years later, his dreams of striking it rich in America in stark contrast with reality. He had little to show for his efforts other than odd jobs and jail time in both the U.S. and Canada. He now faced imminent bankruptcy. He had a wife to support and a father-in-law demanding repayment of the loan for his latest get-rich-quick scheme—a business directory.

But the money for the directory was gone, and he'd have to go back to the drudgery of working for someone else for a pittance. Trouble was, they never paid him enough to support the lifestyle he deserved. He sighed. Why couldn't he get a break?

Ponzi lovingly extracted his gold pocket watch from his tweed jacket and flipped it open. Ten minutes until the furniture store man came to re-possess his rented office furniture. He was already behind on his payments by several months and had run out of excuses. The upside to the furniture being gone was that he no longer had to move it when the landlord evicted him for his unpaid rent.

In a few hours, he would face Rose's father at dinner. Mr. Gnecco's already low opinion of him would experience a further decline. The Trader's Guide had been a sure thing—a free foreign trade publication that earned its revenues from business advertising. With cheaper rates than the competition, he had been sure companies would come running. The ads hadn't materialized—instead he had received only a half dozen U.S. replies and one from faraway Spain. Worse still, the Spanish reply had mailed him something called an International Postal Reply Coupon instead of the required cash.

He picked up the coupon and studied it. The Spanish was close enough to his native Italian for him to understand that he could redeem the 30 centavos coupon for 5 cents at any U.S. post office.

Peanuts.

Broke or not, a nickel was hardly worth a trip to the post office. He crumpled the paper in his palm and tossed it into his soon to be re-possessed wastebasket.

As he stared at the trashcan, his brain automatically computed the numbers. Thirty centavos for a nickel was a 6-to-1 exchange rate. Did he read that correctly?

His pulse quickened as he picked up the Boston Herald from his desk and flipped to the business pages. He opened to the currency page and traced his finger down the narrow column. Halfway down in tiny print was the Spanish peseta, at a rate of 6.6 to one U.S. dollar. He quickly redid the math. The exchange rate on the international reply coupon was 10% better than the rate in the Boston Herald. He could get 5 cents from the post office, when the going rate was only 4.5 cents.

Five cents for thirty centavos. One IRC wasn't worth a trip, but 10 percent of a bigger amount could make it worthwhile. How could he get more coupons?

Ponzi shot out of his chair and retrieved the crumpled coupon from the trash. He unfolded it and read it carefully. Sure enough, the coupon stated it was redeemable for 5 cents, and that the rate was fixed by international treaty. Irrelevant, since he didn't know anyone in Spain.

But if the post office had agreements with Spain, surely it had arrangements with other countries. Was there such an agreement with Italy? All of Europe had sunk into a depression after the war, none more so than Italy. If Spain had a currency difference, so would Italy. Being born there, he knew people in Italy. People who could help him make money. Boatloads of money.

The Securities Exchange Company, Boston MA—1918

Charles Ponzi was born Carlo Ponzi in Parma, Italy in 1882. He arrived in Boston in 1903, stating that he "landed in this country with $2.50 in cash and $1 million in hopes, and those hopes never left me." It is difficult to verify his claim that he gambled away most of his money on the voyage to America, given his penchant for stretching the truth. What we do know is that he was constantly on the lookout for easy money.

Working for someone else was not his idea of a satisfactory career. After an entry-level job as a dishwasher, he worked briefly as a waiter. He was soon fired for stealing and shortchanging customers. He worked a variety of jobs, but never seemed to last anywhere. The backbreaking life of a laborer was not for him.

A stroke of luck landed him a job at the Bank Zarossi in Montreal, where he had moved in 1907. The bank served Montreal's large immigrant population. Its founder, Luigi "Louis" Zarossi, probably served as Ponzi's inspiration. Zarossi paid depositors 6% interest—twice the market rate at the time. It turns out that Zarossi paid the interest out of new depositors' funds. Maybe what we now call a Ponzi scheme should be called a "Zarossi scheme." The fact that Zarossi named his bank after himself was probably a warning sign of things to come.

Zarossi escaped to Mexico with most of the bank's money, leaving his family behind and destitute. Ponzi probably never imagined he would do something similar a few years later. Or perhaps, in the back of his mind, he believed that if he ever did such a thing, he'd be far more clever.

Once Zarossi's scheme was discovered, Ponzi found himself penniless and out of a job. He wanted to return to the United States but needed money to get there. He visited Zarossi bank customer Canadian Warehousing, no doubt to perpetuate some sort of fraudulent scheme. To his surprise, the office was empty and a company checkbook sat unattended on a desk. Always the opportunist, he proceeded to capitalize on his good fortune by writing a check to himself and forging the signature of a company director. Cashing the check earned him a three-year prison sentence. His impulsive and reckless behavior always seemed to catch up with him.

Ponzi was released from prison in 1911 after serving his sentence. He returned to the U.S. and immediately became involved in smuggling illegal Italian immigrants into the country. This crime resulted in another two-year prison sentence.

In Boston, he met his future wife, Rose Maria Gnecco, and also came up with an idea to sell advertising in a business directory. His idea received only a lukewarm response from most businesses, but one of the respondents was a Spanish company that enclosed an International Reply Coupon (IRC).

Ponzi was intrigued by the fact that the coupon would allow him to buy the equivalent postage needed to post a letter, regardless of the strength of that country's currency. For example, the price of the IRC was much lower in Spain, yet it bought U.S. stamps at a much higher value than what the Spanish company had paid for it. In essence, he could buy these IRCs at a cheaper price in one country and sell them for a higher price in another. This simple arbitrage on currency fluctuations could be his ticket to riches.

Ponzi sent borrowed money to his Italian relatives to buy IRC coupons to send to him. Once he had the coupons in hand, he found that the bureaucratic red tape to redeem them made it hardly worth the effort. However, if he cashed enough of them, it would make the scheme worthwhile. Of course scaling the idea meant getting other investors to give him money.

Other investors had to provide the capital, since it was almost impossible for him to obtain financing. The banks turned him down due to his shady history, lack of a job and no collateral. He also insisted on keeping the details of his plan a secret, so no one else could move in on his surefire way to get rich. A bank loan meant he would have to divulge his money-making plans. Whomever he told might steal his idea.

He decided instead that it would be easy enough to raise small amounts of money from many different investors, as long as he tempted them with generous enough returns. If he made the investment small enough, they wouldn't ask too many questions.

Ponzi did not want to use his own name. Someone might research his background and find out he was an ex-con. He also needed a company name to project the right image of stability and credibility.

A corporation was impossible, because he couldn't afford a lawyer. That left a partnership, but he couldn't risk sharing his idea with anyone. So the *Securities Exchange Company* was born, a "partner-less" partnership, he liked to call it. Except when he filled out the form at Boston City Hall, the registration form required him to list a partner. After a moment's thought he listed his uncle, John S. Dondero, confident Uncle John would never find out.

Now that his company was registered, he set about finding investors to finance the purchase of the IRCs. He raised small amounts at first, ten dollars or so by issuing promissory notes with a return of 10% in just 90 days.

Whatever talent Ponzi lacked in financial acumen, he more than made up for in his understanding of human nature. The mere mention of something as exotic as foreign exchange always drew interest, and adding a 50% return made it irresistible.

He soon employed agents to sell his investments,

promising them a 10% cut. There were no regulations to follow, as the Securities and Exchange Commission would not exist until a few years later in 1921. It was an easy sell; small amounts easy enough to take a chance on, and the potential payoff caught people's attention. In Ponzi's own words:

"It might have looked economically unsound as an investment. But it was extremely attractive as a gamble."

All he needed were the coupons. That was easily achieved with the help of a friend working on a transatlantic liner. Sure enough, the coupons were available. At this point, nothing was illegal. Once Ponzi's friend brought the coupons from Italy, he simply redeemed the coupons and returned the money to his investors, as promised.

Of course, they all wanted to reinvest. So did multitudes of new investors, eager to get rich. When the early investors reaped the profits, word spread quickly. This word of mouth was exactly what Ponzi was counting on. Many more investors lined up with their money, and repeat investors increased their stakes. Rather than $10 or $20, many invested all their savings and even took out loans.

Ponzi's cash grew exponentially. In February 1920, the first month of operations, he brought in $5,000. One month later, it increased to $30,000, and just a couple of months after that, $420,000. By July, he was making millions, especially after a flattering article in the *Boston Post* in late July 1920. That article changed his life. Thousands came to the Niles Building, eager to invest with him.

Charles Ponzi—Not the First, Or the Last

July 24, 1920 was unlike any other Saturday Ponzi had ever seen. Huge crowds gathered outside 27 School Street after the Boston Post story about Ponzi and his Securities Exchange Company. It seemed to him that almost all of Greater Boston's two million inhabitants waited outside the building, anxious to get a piece of his lucrative postal reply coupon business. Policemen on horseback held the crowd in check. He was now bringing in a quarter of a million dollars per day. What a difference from only a few months ago when he was broke and down on his luck.

Unfortunately for Ponzi, it also attracted the attention of some skeptics, including Richard Grozier and Eddie Dunn, the acting publisher and editor, respectively, of the *Post.* They decided to dig deeper and enlisted the services of Clarence Barron, of *Barron's* financial paper fame, to provide a financial analysis and opinion of the likelihood of Ponzi's claimed return on investment.

On July 26th, the Boston Post ran a follow-up article. It was less than complimentary. Barron noted the fact that Ponzi was not investing his own money in the Securities Exchange Company. If it was such a great investment, why didn't he invest alongside his shareholders?

Barron also concluded that since there were only 27,000 postal reply coupons in circulation, Ponzi's numbers didn't add up. He would need to have at least 160 million in circulation to cover his purported investment returns.

That didn't stop the crowds from gathering outside

his office. However, this time exuberance was replaced by anger and panic. Ponzi tried to placate the crowd with coffee and donuts. That, coupled with a dose of his charisma, seemed to work for some, who decided to keep their money invested.

However, both Barron's article and the crowds outside Ponzi's office had caught the attention of Daniel Gallagher, the U.S. Attorney General. He assigned Edwin Pride to audit the Securities Exchange Company.

Ponzi decided the best defense was a good offense. In August 1920, he sued one of the reporters for libel and won a judgment of $500,000. To assuage any doubt about his ability to cash in all the postal reply coupons, he simply stated that his trade secret lay in how he cashed in the coupons. Most believed him. He was invincible.

The immense popularity of the postal reply coupons also brought another set of problems. Even if he could get his hands on enough coupons, the transatlantic return voyage to and from Europe took too long to turn around the investment in the required time frame.

Meanwhile, the audit went on, and Ponzi continued to insist his success lay in his secret methodology. He temporarily closed the company to new investments, using the audit as an excuse. He also hired a publicity agent, William McMasters, who was a former reporter.

It is difficult to determine exactly when Ponzi stopped buying the international reply coupons. At whatever point he stopped buying them, the scheme became a fraud. Eventually though, it became obvious to others besides Barron that there simply weren't enough international postal reply coupons in global circulation to provide the returns to the multitudes of new investors.

The audit also turned up irregularities, the most egregious of which was the lack of an adequate bookkeeping system. Ponzi had no accounting system whatsoever. His records consisted of investor names printed on index cards, which was a huge red flag.

It wasn't only a few journalists and non-investors who became suspicious. William McMasters, the publicity agent, was shocked at Ponzi's deplorable lack of financial knowledge, given that he purported to be a financial genius. A little digging confirmed his suspicions that all was not as Ponzi would have him believe. Rather than raking in the profits, Ponzi was actually in the hole for at least $4.5 million.

McMasters, another opportunist, sold his story to the *Post* for $5,000. The story caused a run on redemptions, but Ponzi somehow managed to meet them.

Meanwhile, the U.S. Attorney's audit uncovered even more startling discrepancies. Ponzi was more than $7 million in debt. Matters only deteriorated further when the *Post* discovered Ponzi's Canadian criminal record and jail time. The same day the *Post* revealed Ponzi's criminal record, the Bank Commission seized Hanover Trust, a bank Ponzi had previously taken over with his millions.

In all, Ponzi's scheme caused the failure of six banks and losses of more than $20 million. He was arrested and charged with mail fraud. He pleaded guilty in exchange for a lighter sentence of only five years, but served only three-and-a-half years. That was not the end of his troubles, however. Once released from federal prison, the state of Massachusetts brought charges against him. He was too broke to hire a lawyer to defend himself against the 22 charges of larceny, so he represented himself. He used his charm to beat the first ten counts in his first of three trials.

His next two trials were not as favorable. His second trial was deadlocked. At the third state trial he was convicted and sentenced to seven to nine years in prison.

While still out on bail, he hatched another scheme, selling swampland in Florida under the company name Charpon (formed from letters of his first and last name). Once found out, he tried to flee to Italy aboard a transatlantic ship. However, he was apprehended at the ship's last U.S. port of call in New Orleans. He had his bail revoked and was shipped off to prison to serve the rest of his term.

Upon Ponzi's release in 1934, he was immediately deported to Italy. He eventually landed a job with Ala Littoria, an Italian airline. The position was based in Brazil, but that ended with World War II, when flights to Brazil ceased. By his own account, he made $15 million in nine months, only to lose it all in the end.

His wife Rose finally divorced him, and his health declined after a stroke. Ponzi's fall from grace was even more rapid than his rise to fame and fortune. He spent the last years of his life in Rio de Janeiro, where he died alone and in poverty on January 18, 1949.

CHAPTER 4

NINETEENTH CENTURY SWINDLERS— PONZI PIONEERS

Boston's Scollay Square, circa 1887 (PD-US)

A New Era

NINETEENTH-CENTURY AMERICA WAS AN INTERESTING place. Commerce boomed as America expanded westward. Stock trading multiplied six-fold, yet banking crises occurred almost as frequently as presidential elections. The women's suffrage movement gathered steam, and a great influx of immigrants began to shape the country that exists today. Society transformed from mainly agricultural to manufacturing-based as people flocked to the cities.

The late 1800s also marked the rise of commerce in America. It was an era where the nouveau riche thrived but the masses barely survived. Whether you met with opportunity or misfortune, there was no social safety net. Individuals had to be creative to make ends meet. Along with entrepreneurs came shady opportunists eager to separate the newly affluent from their money. The criminal types not only targeted the rich but ordinary people as well. Anyone eager to earn an outsized return on his hard-won wages and savings was fair game. One particularly successful scammer was a woman named Sarah Howe.

Sarah Howe and the Ladies Deposit Company

Ponzi Particulars	Sarah Howe
Theme	The Ladies Deposit Company
Fraud	$500,000 ($11 million in today's dollars)
Promised return	2% per week
Investors defrauded	1,200 women
Date discovered	1880s
Where	Boston, Massachusetts
Prison sentence	3 years

The Ladies Deposit Company—
Boston, Massachusetts, 1879

Sarah Howe opened her desk drawer and tucked the envelope of cash inside. The late morning sun streamed into her Garland Street office and reflected off the crystal inkwell on her new mahogany table. All the trappings of success: something she never would have dreamed of less than a year ago.

Business was good. She scribbled out a receipt and tore it from the book. She handed it to the woman seated across the desk from her with a smile. "You will be glad you did this."

Edith Clark held out a plump hand, the fabric of her dress straining against her ample midriff as she leaned forward. Tiny rows of intricate buttons from her collar to her waist reflected the chandelier light. Pearl earrings sunk into the plump pillows of her ear lobes. Her dress spoke of household servants, even before she mentioned her physician father. Sarah had checked her background to be doubly sure she was unmarried. Married women were not permitted to deposit funds in her bank for one simple reason: they came with suspicious husbands.

Edith beamed back at her. "I already am. I wish I had more to invest."

"Just remember. Very few can invest in the Ladies Deposit Company. You will keep earning 2% per week as long as you keep it confidential." The success of her venture depended upon total secrecy. Investing too much at once would surely result in unwanted publicity and scrutiny. Though the women were all unmarried, they had watchful fathers and brothers.

"Of course, Mrs. Howe. I won't tell a soul." Edith paused. "I was wondering—my sister Ella also likes to help the needy. Would you be willing to make an exception for her? She's very discreet."

Sarah hesitated. "Normally I wouldn't, but for you..." She sighed. "I'll see what I can do, but you must be patient."

"Oh thank you, Mrs. Howe! I'll tell Ella to get her money ready."

"I can't promise you, but I will try." Sarah patted Edith's arm and steered her to the front hall. "Your generosity will be rewarded very soon. Helping the less fortunate is a very noble cause."

Sarah always got the money before she gave

the whole pitch. She claimed the money went to a Quaker charity that financed payments to the poor. The Ladies Deposit Company supposedly lent money to the Quaker fund. In return, the female depositors received very generous interest payments. The fact that she immediately paid them three months' interest in advance always sealed the deal.

Sarah neglected to mention that she would be the one helped most of all. Instead of disclosing any further details, she opened her front door and showed the woman out. She despised prolonging small talk with these dull women. They had more money than they deserved, sailing through life without hardship. It was so unlike the hardscrabble existence she had endured at their age.

She did, however, like the fact that they hung on her every word, especially when she mentioned the interest payments. Two percent a week was enough to gain anyone's attention. Rather than worrying about handing their cash over, their focus shifted to earning the same return on the rest of their money. Edith Clark was just one of the many women who let their greed lead them.

Sarah always insisted on a low deposit to start. The small amount helped ensure her scheme didn't arouse suspicion. Once she had their trust, she happily allowed them to invest more.

She felt no guilt taking their money. Most of the investors came from affluent backgrounds or had good jobs as schoolteachers and such. Almost all would be married within a few years anyway. It was money they could afford to lose.

Charles Ponzi—Not the First, Or the Last

Unlike her. After losing her husband in her twenties, she had struggled to make ends meet. Without the benefit of an education, she did whatever she could to earn a living. Her previous livelihood of fortune telling had provided a steady income, but she found the endless tales of loves lost or family woes rather tiresome and depressing. Nevertheless, that stream of visitors had provided the seed for her women's investment bank.

These women would never miss the money, and since they couldn't withdraw it on demand, she didn't have to worry about a run on the bank. She knew none wanted to forsake the hefty interest payments.

The idea of providing loans to poor women appealed to them also. If they felt any guilt at all about their fortunate financial circumstances, they could rationalize that their investment earnings also helped the needy. How long did she need to keep this plan of hers going? Not for much longer, the way the money was coming in. In just a few more weeks she'd have enough to start a new life somewhere, far away from Boston.

This business was easier than taking candy from a baby. It was her best idea yet and she only wished she had thought of it sooner. She hadn't even advertised. Word of mouth had spread like wildfire throughout the parlors and kitchens of Boston as women waited for the exclusive invitation to hand over their cash. Day in, day out, she took in thousands of dollars from women anxious to squirrel away savings.

She was very careful to ensure the women met the criteria. Her strict rules not only kept her solvent, they also eliminated awkward questions about money she had no intention of returning.

Her depositors knew better than to tell authorities. One mention to anyone and they would be cut out of the lucrative investment scheme and not be allowed to invest again. Those were the rules, and Sarah made sure they understood them. The rules were necessary to keep the money rolling in. As long as she kept it going, she'd never have to work again.

Undone

Despite her best efforts, Sarah soon attracted attention. Within a year, she had purchased a $50,000 mansion at No 2 East Brookline Street with $20,000 in cash as a down payment. How could a single woman do that?

She also earned the nickname "Old Eight Percent." To be a successful female financier was quite an accomplishment in an age where women did not even have the right to vote and were still considered a man's chattel or property. Women were not only considered inferior, but also helpless without a man to guide them. They certainly couldn't manage money—at least that was the general consensus in that era.

It wouldn't be long before Howe's nickname changed to "The Woman's Bank Swindler." In an age when women were assumed unable to understand complex financial transactions, how could it be that a woman would be running her own bank?

That did not concern the maids and schoolteachers that flocked to deposit their money with Howe. They were just happy to hand over their money for an investment that paid eight percent per month. It practically doubled their investment in just a year. Since it was by referral only, it imparted an air of exclusivity. Soon 1,200 women had deposited over $500,000.

A condition of investment was secrecy, which effectively kept her scheme under the radar from authorities. Still, word eventually spread that the banker was a former fortune-teller. Her former job probably allowed her to easily spot victims. Prior to that, she had even masqueraded as a physician, despite no qualifications.

The *Ladies Deposit* had one particularly innovative feature. The depositors were only able to withdraw the interest portion of their funds. This prevented a run on redemptions and ensured Howe could keep the bulk of the cash for herself without any questions.

What woman wouldn't want to try her hand at investing? Squirreling away a bit of cash appealed to Howe's victims. It was an early American example of affinity fraud.

Affinity fraud targets a group that has similarities to the fraudster by playing on the common bonds that exist between these people. The common thread could be religion, ethnicity, or in this case, gender. We feel an implicit bond with people similar to ourselves. In Howe's case, it was particularly effective, since in the 1880s women were marginalized and had little or no other investing alternatives. In a way, Howes had cornered the market. While the individual amounts scammed from each woman were small, her customer base was exclusive and practically limitless.

Charles Ponzi—Not the First, Or the Last

The first sign of trouble came in 1880, less than a year after she had started the fund. A "run" on the bank began as word spread that the *Ladies Deposit* was a scam. She was exposed by the *Boston Daily Advertiser*, who claimed her scheme had no method of earning returns, and no basis to pay the interest. Investors demanded their money back.

To prove them wrong, Howe paid out all claims, amounting to $150,000 in interest and about $90,000 in principal. But it was too late. Soon after, she was unable to pay interest as it became due, and the *Ladies Deposit* became insolvent, bilking more than 800 investors out of almost $300,000.

She was charged with four counts of fraud and served three years in prison.

While Howe's scam seemed to reinforce that women were incapable of managing their financial affairs, Howe appeared to prove them wrong in the end.

Shortly after being released from prison, she started an identical scam, this time promising a return of seven percent per month. Once caught, she still managed to abscond with $50,000 and was never heard from again.

William Miller aka Bill "520 Percent" Miller

Ponzi Particulars	Bill "520 Percent" Miller
Theme	The Franklin Syndicate, insider stock trading
Fraud	$1 million
Promised return	10% per week
Investors defrauded	Thousands
Date discovered	1899
Where	Brooklyn, New York
Prison sentence	10 years, pardoned after 5

Charles Ponzi—Not the First, Or the Last

The Franklin Syndicate, Brooklyn, New York, 1899

Bill Miller shivered and fastened the top button of his coat. It was early afternoon on Friday, November 24, 1899. He walked briskly, headed to his lawyer's office in Manhattan after an unsettled morning at his Brooklyn office. The sun peeked through the clouds as a cold wind whipped up the leaves around his feet. But the chill in the air was not just from the weather.

Less than two years ago, he had been earning a bookkeeper's salary of only $15 a week; now here he was, a twenty-something entrepreneur seeking a lawyer's advice about millions of dollars.

On the Promenade, Brooklyn Bridge, New York,
Copyright 1899 by Strohmeyer & Wyman.

Courtesy Library of Congress

Before founding the Franklin Syndicate two years ago, he could never have imagined being in such circumstances today. Nor had he ever considered a problem as big as the one he faced now. His sudden great fortune now rested on the cusp of an equally abrupt undoing. As the weather had changed, so had investor sentiment. A chill was in the air, and it was too late to turn back the growing rumblings and doubt that rippled through the city.

His reversal of fortune had started at eleven this morning with a simple payment request. Stories had been circulating for weeks that the Franklin Syndicate was "shaky" and that the weekly 10% returns were too good to be true.

The premise for the Franklin Syndicate was simple. Miller advertised that he had an "inside track" on Wall Street, a way to make returns no one else could. Most people bought into his promise of outsized profits. None of the investors doubted the goose that laid the golden egg—doing so branded them as fools.

The few naysayers were quickly ridiculed by the masses. Even negative newspaper accounts had not deterred investors. Rather, their confidence increased when they received their 10% "dividends." Most reinvested the proceeds. Today, a few of the two thousand people who had invested with him stood outside the Franklin Syndicate offices at 144 Floyd Street ready to withdraw their funds. The crowd's buoyant mood remained un-swayed by the naysayers. Most investors waited patiently to deposit more, often everything they had.

Many of the investors lived and worked near the

Franklin Syndicate office in the German district of Brooklyn. They invested after having seen first-hand the investment returns of their neighbors and friends. Soon investors came from farther afield, like Manhattan and its environs. Some investors came from as far away as California, as Miller's advertising attracted more investors.

But the end of the scheme was only a matter of time—he felt it in his bones. To pay the multitudes of new investors he had to either raise more cash, or delay payments.

The crowd's mood darkened an hour after opening, when a man demanded immediate redemption of his investment. Miller refused, but he could not silence the man's angry protests. A pall dampened the crowd's earlier optimism, as more people around the man took notice of his accusations.

Miller had taken to requiring one week's notice for any withdrawals, despite the fact that only the recent notes required this notice period. The early notes specified immediate payment, and this man had presented a note for immediate payment. When Miller handed him a slip for shares of stock instead, the crowd became uneasy. Others also demanded repayment. While they amounted to only about one hundred people out of the thousands who invested, it was a sharp reversal from earlier days, almost like a "run on the bank."

But there wasn't enough money, at least not on the premises. All funds deposited to date were with his lawyer, Robert A. Ammon. Today's receipts had been about $15,000, of which he had instructed his brother to hide $8,500 under a sofa next door at the apartment of his employee, Miss Anna Gorley.

He couldn't return the money even if he wanted to. There was no ten percent weekly return, no "inside track" on the stock market that generated the outsized returns. And the banks had refused to lend him any more money, suspicious of his ten percent returns.

Reversal of fortune

While Miller hadn't expected his good fortune to last, he never expected it to end quite so soon, either. In just under two years, the Franklin Syndicate had become so successful that he had hired staff and expanded his Brooklyn office from a single room at 144 Floyd Street to the entire upper floor.

His mountain of wealth began to crumble as word of his new redemption policy spread throughout the city. Earlier this afternoon, The Broadway Bank in New York closed his account, stating that the ten percent returns were impossible. The Hide and Leather Bank followed suit, suspicious because his dividend payments were paid in cash, not by check. Without checks, there was no way to trace or reconcile the payments back to each investor.

Other banks were also suspicious, and he had been unable to find one to lend him any money. Without the money, the Franklin Syndicate could not last another day. Most of the hundreds of people who had lined up outside his office this morning to deposit were now looking to cash in, thanks to the banks' unfavorable comments.

Miller could not argue with their conclusions,

because he was pocketing a good portion of the money for himself. These now insurmountable problems brought him to the law office of Robert A. Ammon, before his signature on the assignment of funds barely had time to dry. His lawyer held his funds and promised that everything would be resolved.

Turning over what remained of the money for Ammon to hold in trust might stop the detectives from chasing him. He had managed to evade them for a couple of days, but he couldn't hide from the authorities forever. They had staked out his offices, house and everything in between.

Miller and Ammon's plan was simple: Miller would leave the city, and Ammon would hand over the assignment to allow the authorities to liquidate The Franklin Syndicate. Prior to doing that, however, they had both secreted away a tidy sum for later. They would split the money, once all the fuss died down.

Miller fingered the train ticket in his pocket as he exited the street and opened the door to Ammon's office. One way to Montreal, leaving tonight. That gave him the weekend as a head start before the Franklin Syndicate offices reopened on Monday, and Ammon handed over the assignment of assets to the police.

Aftermath

Miller was apprehended in Montreal within a few days. He was returned to await trial, and on April 30, 1900, was sentenced to ten years at Sing Sing prison.

His story did not end with his arrest and conviction. Like a true con, he had one more ace up his sleeve.

While in prison Miller had contracted tuberculosis,

or consumption as it was called back then. With seven years left on his sentence and the possibility of dying before release, he had second thoughts about the cash he had left with Ammon, his lawyer. Why should his lawyer live scot-free with all that money?

Had Ammon truly defended him to the fullest, or had it been a half-hearted attempt? Miller realized now that Ammon had a conflict of interest. Making Miller a scapegoat meant Ammon was free to do as he pleased—and spend the money.

Ammon also had not provided Miller's family with the payments they had agreed upon when they hid $240,000 of investor money. Miller had serious concerns about Mrs. Ammon's real estate purchases around the city. Was Ammon diverting his money to fund real estate investments under her name?

In May 1903, he decided to expose his two partners in crime, Ammon and Edward Schlessinger. Schlessinger was a business agent who steered investors to The Franklin Syndicate in exchange for a cut.

After Miller began singing like a canary, Ammon was convicted and joined Miller at Sing Sing, but Schlessinger managed to escape to Europe with $150,000—enough to live comfortably for the rest of his life.

Miller did not serve his full sentence. After five years, he successfully obtained a pardon. Upon his release, he opened a grocery store on Long Island and soon got a new nickname: Honest Bill.

CHAPTER 5

PONZI COUNTDOWN—PONZI #10—PAUL BURKS

Ponzi Particulars	Paul Burks
Theme	ZeekRewards, penny auction website
Fraud	$600 million
Promised return	1.5% per day
Investors defrauded	1 million +
Date discovered	2012
Where	Lexington, North Carolina
Prison sentence	None to date

ZeekRewards, Lexington, North Carolina—August 2012

PAUL BURKS SLIPPED INTO HIS office and quietly closed the door, exhausted. A steady stream of investors flowed through his Center Street office all day long. The constant traffic and repeated slamming of the front door gave him a headache. Headaches plagued him often these days. Usually the pain was worth it, given that the high number of visitors was good news.

When the door slammed this time, however, it was a delivery from the U.S. Postal Service. The letter carrier usually brought big bundles of mail wrapped with thick elastic bands. Lately though, Burks had noticed a change. There were fewer envelopes, and those he did receive were more likely to contain redemption requests instead of investment checks.

Fewer deposits meant less cash to pay for the increased redemption requests. He leaned back in his chair and clasped his hands behind his head.

He needed a good reason to stall paying them without raising alarm bells. That was a challenge, given that most everyone in Lexington, North Carolina was an investor, and news of any delays traveled fast.

Most of the eighteen thousand citizens of this sleepy town had either invested in ZeekRewards, knew of someone who had, or wanted to invest. People waited to accost him whenever he ventured out of the office, whether he was heading to the Village Grill for lunch or on his way home. He couldn't possibly talk to all of them. He avoided them as much as he could, insisting each individual contact the office directly instead. He had become especially elusive now that more people were asking for their money back.

He couldn't even grocery shop without hostile looks from the cashier or shoppers in the checkout line, a far cry from the fawning attention he had received only months ago.

ZeekRewards had grown far beyond his wildest dreams. It was now too big, and there was no longer enough cash to keep it going. He had done his best. Was it his fault that people practically tripped over themselves, begging to get in?

No, it was not.

They had only themselves to blame. He had set a limit of $10,000 per person, but people still invested more, often under the name of a friend or relative. They did that on their own, and he made no effort to stop them.

His rule was actually quite effective. Rather than limit the amount, it had exactly the opposite effect. People rushed to invest, worried that only a limited number of people could get in, especially since the investment amount was capped. Word spread quickly that time was of the essence if you wanted in on the action. Who wouldn't want to earn 1.5% per day for a few minutes' work?

No, as far as he was concerned, any money troubles were their own fault. They should not have invested funds they could not afford to lose. While he felt sorry for them, what could he do? Maybe this would teach them a lesson about investing beyond their means.

The Scheme

Zeekler.com started in 2010 as a penny auction site. Bidders could win items at ridiculously low prices, but there was a catch. While bidders could bid on—and win—an iPad or computer sometimes 90% lower than retail, they had to pay for each of their bids.

Customers bought a package of bids when they first signed up, and they used these to bid on items. Bid sales added up quickly. The items at auction were designed to be too good to be true on purpose, to attract the maximum number of bidders. Almost all items required multiple bids from each bidder, and it was easy for bidders to get caught up in the action. The dollars added up very quickly before a bidder realized it.

Bidders also bought bids for later use. Since their bids were pre-purchased, it was easy to forget how much equivalent money those bids represented. Once an initial bid was made, investors already felt "invested" by lower bids. It was a psychological ploy to encourage additional bids to stay in the game.

The auctioned item was more of a loss leader. While there could be only one winner, the multiple bids from each bidder added up to a tidy sum. The penny auction site made money not from the item for sale, but on the sale of the bids themselves. The end result was that bid revenue far surpassed any profits gained from the sale of the item itself, which often sold at a loss.

For everyone but the winners, the money spent on unsuccessful bids was gone forever once the auction ended. Unless you had the winning bid, you walked away empty-handed. No new iPad for you. Just less cash, or prepaid bids, in your account.

And if you were the lucky winner? The formula was so complicated that it was hard to know what you actually had paid for the item you won. Was it one bid or more? How many times did you outbid another person? That iPad cost you not only what you bid, but the cost of the multiple bids you purchased to bid on it. It was expensive, and as addictive as gambling. Getting caught up in the bidding meant you could easily spend more on bids than what the item was worth, yet still lose out.

Burks didn't stop with only the one investment idea. He offered another deal. People could invest in the penny auction site itself and take a share of the profits. The investors in the site turned out to be the biggest losers of all.

ZeekRewards was the investment side of the

scheme. For an investment of up to $10,000 in ZeekRewards, Burks promised investors a share in the daily profits of the Zeekler.com penny auction site. Some people even mortgaged their houses or borrowed funds for the right to share in up to 50% of the penny auction site's daily profits. The "profits" were paid in "profit points", rather than actual cash. The "profit points" calculation was a complicated formula, usually approximating a 1.5% return to the investor.

All an investor had to do to earn profit points was to promote ZeekRewards on other websites and recruit others. In less than two years, the number of investors surpassed a million.

At first, Burks allowed investors to redeem their points for cash. As the amounts owed to investors grew, however, he realized the large redemptions could have a significant impact on his cash flow. He changed the rules, requiring investors to give advance notice of redemptions.

The complicated formula and the advance notice were both important features. They prevented spontaneous redemptions and allowed Burks to cover his tracks to perpetuate the scheme.

Many of Burks' investors were fanatics, believing him to be a "genius." They fervently believed he had transformed their lives, at least until ZeekRewards came crashing down. ZeekRewards worked similar to multi-level marketing sales pitches, only without the work of actively recruiting people below you. Instead, you simply had to place an ad and let the people join of their own accord.

Prior to ZeekRewards, Burks had worked in multi-level marketing jobs for most of his career. Before that, he had started several other companies. Those companies were ultimately suspended after each failed to comply with state reporting requirements.

Burks had also run for the state House as a member of the Libertarian party, ironically stating during his campaign that as a Libertarian, his quest would be "to reduce the government in every place that's possible." No doubt, he included the North Carolina Attorney General and the SEC in his vision.

He not only failed to get elected to office, but came in last with only a few hundred votes.

In his earlier years, he had practiced his sleight of hand, ironically enough, as a magician touring nursing homes.

Red Flags

Signs that things were about to end came on Friday, August 17, 2012. Burks' Lexington office closed and the ZeekRewards website went down. It was an ominous portent. Later that evening, the SEC finally shut ZeekRewards down.

After years of complaints and accusations, the Securities and Exchange Commission finally launched a lawsuit against ZeekRewards. The lawsuit alleged that Burks took in $600 million from more than one million investors by offering and selling securities in an unregistered pyramid and Ponzi scheme.

Burks claimed that rather than selling unregistered securities, ZeekRewards was selling e-commerce sub-scriptions. He required investors to sign a statement that they "were not purchasing stock or any form of investment or equity" in order to become members. However, every other communication implies otherwise. You can find many YouTube videos on Zeekler and Paul Burks touting the fantastic returns.

Complaints and inquiries about the legitimacy of the operation grew. The Winston-Salem Better Business Bureau fielded almost 30,000 Zeeks calls in the days after the SEC action, more than any other company in history.

The North Carolina Attorney General's office had received complaints, but forwarded them to the Secretary of State's office because the business seemed to involve securities. The confusion over jurisdiction allowed Zeeks to operate longer than it should have.

Finally, in August 2012, ZeekRewards was forced into receivership by the North Carolina court. Given the more than one million investors, recovery efforts will be lengthy and time-consuming. Net "winners" will need to have their returns re-apportioned amongst those who had not received any "profits." As with all Ponzi schemes, all transactions must be unwound, in order to calculate proportionate amounts owed to each investor.

No criminal charges have been filed to date, and Burks paid a fine of $4 million to the SEC without any admission of guilt. He got off easy: the $4 million was simply the amount of money still in his possession.

While Burks' scheme was not the largest in terms of dollars, it certainly was the largest in U.S. history by sheer numbers of investors. Over a million people were duped, buying into the idea that they could parlay their $10,000 investment into a fortune with the promised 10% interest per week.

Had these investors done their homework, they would have realized it was not only impossible to pay that sort of return, but that it defied logic as well. If the auction business was really that lucrative, Burks would have had a myriad of alternate financing options to choose from. He would not have had to source cash from millions of small investors. Any bank would have jumped at the chance to lend the money at a far lower return than 1.5% a day. Of course, banks would have insisted on a few minor details such as audited financial statements. Simple math and common sense provided the answer, had anyone cared to look.

Instead, people were motivated by greed. They rushed to get in on a sure thing without checking the facts. They simply did not want to miss out.

There were earlier signs that something was amiss. In May 2012, during the U.S. Memorial Day weekend, ZeekRewards announced that any check holders must immediately cash their checks, because the company was switching banks. Any outstanding checks not cashed would have to be re-issued.

The timing of the announcement was interesting, given that it was a U.S. holiday. Press releases issued on a weekend are far less likely to receive scrutiny from news agencies and regulators. For this reason, companies and governments often time the release of bad news for the weekend, hoping the information will get buried under other news. At the very least, any weekend news will be disseminated and digested before Monday morning. Was Zeeks trying to pass this under the radar?

The ZeekRewards announcement claimed that their two current banks, New Bridge Bank and BB&T, could not handle their banking needs. The announcement was vague on the reasons why these large and established financial institutions were inadequate. Could it be because the FDIC banks were asking questions, or were required to disclose transactions if asked? If these banks couldn't handle the lucrative business that Zeeks purported to run, who could?

Zeeks warned that all transactions needed to clear the banks by June 1, 2012. People had less than a week to not only deposit their payment checks, but also to have them clear. Companies generally do not shut down their bank accounts before all transactions have cleared. Normally they slowly transition from the old account to the new, only closing the original bank account once all the transactions have cleared. There is no need to notify people. The sense of urgency for the commission holders was another sign something was amiss.

A third red flag was the new financial arrangements. They were not through a brick-and-mortar bank. Instead, investors were directed to send payments to offshore payment providers AlertPay and SolidTrustPay. These payment providers allow companies to be less transparent and potentially make the assets harder to trace and seize.

Were these steps taken to escape scrutiny, or

perhaps prevent seizure of assets by US authorities? I think we know the answer.

Aftermath

Ken Bell, the court-appointed receiver, is still determining the final distribution to investors. No one knows exactly how much money Burks took in, or the exact number of investors (Ponzi schemers are notoriously poor bookkeepers). With a million or maybe even two million investors, many of whom had received payments, the sheer volume of transactions make the money very hard to trace. By contrast, Madoff's Ponzi was much bigger but involved only thousands of investors.

Burks' strategy of small amounts with many investors meant that he appealed primarily to unsophisticated investors less likely to scrutinize and analyze the details. The small investment amounts also ensured it would not be cost effective for any individual investor to pursue court action individually.

If investors are extremely lucky, they might receive half of their money back. As of summer 2013, the wind-up and distribution of the money was still underway.

www.zeekler.com no longer exists, and how Paul Burks spends his days right now is unknown.

CHAPTER 6

PONZI #9—MARC DREIER

Ponzi Particulars	Marc Dreier
Theme	Dreier LLP, forged short-term promissory notes
Fraud	$750 Million
Promised return	Up to 11.5%
Investors defrauded	800+
Date discovered	2008
Where	New York
Prison sentence	150 years

Stamford, Connecticut—October 2008

MARC DREIER AND HIS PARTNER in crime, Kosta Kovachev, sat across from two hedge fund managers in the glass-walled conference room at Solow Realty. If all went well, they could appease the investors and put off their demands for immediate repayment on the overdue Solow Realty promissory notes. The notes had matured, but Dreier knew Solow Realty wouldn't be paying the money back anytime soon.

Solow's management had no idea the notes even existed. Dreier had passed off the forged promissory notes as issued by Solow Realty. He had even provided a doctored copy of Solow Realty's audited financial statements as backup for the loans.

The Solow Realty promissory notes were fabricated,

an elaborate ruse solely designed to enrich Dreier. He marketed and sold primarily to hedge funds, which were easily seduced by the high returns. He met investors at Solow's offices, masquerading as Solow's chief executive officer. He then provided the notes in exchange for the investor's cash.

He was confident he could pull it off, as long as Solow management didn't discover he was up to no good. Dreier, a lawyer, provided legal services to Solow and so was a frequent visitor at the Solow office. Seeing a familiar face, the receptionist just waved him in with his guests.

Business transacted to date had all been by email or phone, good enough for almost $200 million dollars worth of investment money. The notes were now due, and Dreier had tried unsuccessfully to convince the hedge fund to roll the notes over for another term. Worse still, the hedge fund had demanded an in-person meeting for the first time, at the Solow offices no less.

So here they were, in a high-stakes gamble. Dreier pretended to be Solow CEO Steven Cherniak, while Kovachev impersonated Solow's financial controller. It was a last-ditch attempt to escape detection.

Dreier drew in a deep breath as the other men pulled documents from their briefcases. As long as he and Kovachev stayed with the script they had rehearsed this morning, they could pull off the ruse and hold off the hedge fund. There was no time to waste. Every minute in the Solow offices heightened their risk of discovery.

He froze in mid-sentence as Sheldon Solow, Solow Realty's founder, walked by the conference room.

Solow slowed and peered through the glass wall, staring directly at Dreier, a puzzled look on his face.

Dreier broke into a wide grin and held up a finger as if to say he'd catch up with him in a few minutes. His heart stopped. What if Solow decided to come in the conference room? The hedge fund manager would discover the scheme, and discover exactly why his promissory notes remained unpaid. Luckily, Solow just waved back and resumed his walk down the hall.

All good, thought Dreier. He felt a rush of exhilaration as he realized he was about to get away with his reckless scheme. Solow had no clue about what was going on right under his nose. The billionaire real estate tycoon's days were always filled with back-to-back appointments, so it was unlikely he would retrace his steps to seek Dreier out today. That gave Dreier plenty of time to drum up an excuse for being here with strangers in the Solow conference room. He'd mention a meeting with CEO Cherniak, and pass off the others as some of the other 250 lawyers from Dreier LLP.

His immediate focus was to placate the two guys in front of him and exit Solow's offices before Solow returned. There was no way he could produce the millions needed to redeem the notes. Instead, he focused on getting the hedge fund to roll over these notes into a new, higher-interest note. A promise of even higher returns solved everyone's immediate problems. He spun his most convincing tale to date.

Dreier's Undoing

Dreier managed to get away with his trickery

in Solow's meeting room that day, at least at first. Everything was fine until another hedge fund became suspicious about the notes. That company contacted Solow Realty directly. Dreier was finally exposed.

Meanwhile, Dreier continued his impersonations. The next time he attempted his trickery was in Toronto, Canada, at the offices of the Ontario Teachers' Pension Plan, where he pretended to be an OTPP lawyer in front of still another hedge fund. This time his audacious plan failed. He was arrested.

While in jail, the financial controller for Dreier LLP discovered missing funds in Dreier's bankrupt client 360 Networks' escrow account. Dreier was arrested upon his return to the U.S. and also charged in a civil suit by the SEC. His run with lady luck was finally over.

There were plenty of signs something was amiss in this scheme, however no one cared to acknowledge the problem hiding in plain sight. Greed often blinds people. Everyone in Dreier's orbit benefited from his fraud. The lawyers earned handsome fees, the hedge funds and celebrity clients received outsized returns, and Drier's charities benefited from his large donations.

While 8%-12 % returns were not as stratospheric as some other Ponzi schemes, Dreier knew he had to be careful about being too obvious. He was dealing with sophisticated investment professionals, so he avoided suspicion by offering returns on the high end of the market. They were low enough to avoid questions and high enough to make them more attractive than alternatives for the multitude of hedge funds searching for a decent return.

Ponzi #9—Marc Dreier

Dreier LLP paid lavish compensation to the hundreds of lawyers it employed and the premises were equally opulent. The office walls at 499 Park Place were more like an art gallery than a law office, decorated with expensive original art, including a Picasso. Everything about the place was impressive, just like Dreier himself. Just a few short years after founding the firm, he acquired luxurious homes in the Hamptons, Manhattan, and Santa Monica, and a 121-foot yacht for splashy parties in New York and the Caribbean.

Unlike most law firms, Dreier LLP was not structured as a true partnership. Marc Dreier was the only partner. He was also the only one with complete access to the company's finances. He controlled everything to such an extent that upon his arrest, the firm was paralyzed, unable to pay bills. Ironically, the unpaid invoices included Dreier LLP's malpractice insurance premiums.

Where did it all go wrong? Dreier had always had a promising future. Smart and ambitious, he had a comfortable upbringing on Long Island, and graduated from Yale and then Harvard Law. He made partner quickly, but it wasn't enough. He wanted status, and wouldn't stop until he was the biggest and the best. That meant starting his own firm.

But he felt things weren't happening fast enough. One day he experimented and altered a legal document. It netted him a million dollars, and he was amazed at how easy it was to cheat.

Then in 2004, he pulled off a $20-million fraud. That also escaped detection and at that point,

Dreier never looked back. His frauds crept above the $100-million mark, culminating with the plan to sell $500 million in fake Solow promissory notes to at least three different hedge funds.

As Dreier commented in the documentary *Unraveled*: "It's easy to say you'd never cross the line, but the line is presented to very few people."

In his eyes, a few people refuse to cross the line as a fundamental virtue, but most people do not cross simply because they have not had the opportunity. In other words, he thinks almost everyone would commit fraud if enticed with a lucrative enough opportunity. At least this is how temptation appears to fraudsters; they assume everyone shares the same values (or lack thereof), and computes the same risk/reward trade-off they do.

Dreier would probably repeat his crimes if he could, despite the repercussions he has experienced. His possessions have been auctioned off, except for two valuable paintings that were mysteriously removed from his offices. They have never been recovered, and their whereabouts is unknown. Dreier was sentenced to twenty years for securities fraud, wire fraud, and money laundering. He is due for release in October 2026.

Dreier's Accomplice

Kovachev, also a Harvard alumnus, began his career—ironically—as an attorney with the Security and Exchange Commission's Enforcement Division. He departed in 1986 to work at Morgan Stanley. He worked there for five years until he gave up his broker's license in 2002 after being implicated in an earlier $28-million Ponzi scheme selling timeshares that defrauded 600 investors in 30 states. His lawyer got him a settlement, which included a $350,000 fine with no admission of guilt. His lawyer? Marc Dreier.

Somewhat fascinating is a profile I discovered on LinkedIn.com for a man also named Kosta Kovachev. The LinkedIn profile shows a middle-aged man wearing sunglasses with a fedora pulled down low on his forehead.

He describes himself as a "Renaissance Man" with consulting experience who offers his "Creative Talents to helping Any and All Organizations" (sic). He lists some of his specialties as Business Development and Capital Raising. Missing from his profile is any work experience. However, he appears to have graduated from Harvard Business School in 1982, the same year as Dreier's accomplice. The next accomplishment on his profile is in April 2004, where he lists the position of Managing Director of Arcadia SG until May 2009. Is it the same Kosta Kovachev? There are certainly many parallels. It is hard to be sure since there is no work experience listed from 1982 until the 2004 Arcadia listing. LinkedIn Kovachev worked at Arcadia until May 2009, about the time the Dreier Kovachev associate was charged with conspiracy to commit securities fraud and wire fraud.

The Kosta Kovachev in the Marc Dreier Ponzi scheme was found guilty and sentenced to 46 months in prison in March 2010.

CHAPTER 7

PONZI #8—NEVIN SHAPIRO

Ponzi Particulars	Nevin Shapiro
Theme	Capitol Investment USA, Inc., grocery diverting
Fraud	$930 Million
Promised return	10-26% per year
Investors defrauded	60+
Date discovered	2009
Where	Miami, Florida
Prison sentence	20 years

A Day in the Life, 2010

NEVIN SHAPIRO SLOWLY OPENED HIS eyes only to face the same prison wall, part of the tiny prison cell he shared with another inmate in the low security section of the Butner Federal Correction Facility in Butner, North Carolina.

Same scene, different day. He awoke this way each morning, hoping against hope it was all a bad dream. His cellmate's snoring and the drab walls surrounding him dashed his hopes. His September 2027 release date might as well be a hundred years from now, it was so far into the future.

Every day began the same each morning and ended the same way each night. His days were punctuated by bland meals and programs he considered a waste of his time. Despite the Butner facility's generous visiting policy, he had no visitors.

His life now almost had him believing his old life had never existed. Gone was his Miami mansion with the waterfront pool, his yacht, and his millions. Gone was his old life with all its trappings of wealth and success.

Most noticeably missing were the University of Miami Hurricanes players. The young athletes he had considered friends had turned their backs on him. They had abandoned him, despite the hundreds of thousands he'd lavished upon them at strip clubs, bars and restaurants. He'd arranged parties at Miami hotels and later on his yacht, where a crew waited at their disposal. Over the years, he had helped so many of them. Yet overnight they had disowned him. Ungrateful SOBs, after all he had done for them.

Not that he ever kept score, but when the tables turned and he needed help, where were they? Couldn't they make one little visit or at least call? He already knew the answer. He had been written off, a part of their history they would rather just forget.

Well, he could play that game too. If they weren't willing to help him, he wasn't about to help them keep their secrets, either. The whole ungrateful lot of them deserved punishment.

All the VIP room parties they had on his dime, the bar tabs, hookers, and cash whenever they asked. Now that they had their millions and their mansions, it was easy to downplay his part in their success. His help early on in their careers had provided connections and lucky breaks that led to their multi-million dollar contracts, and kept them out of trouble. He had even arranged an abortion for one player and bought an engagement ring for another, so intertwined was he in their lives.

Now that he could barely afford a snack from the commissary, where were they? Distancing themselves from their dirty laundry. But if he had to live in this hell hole, they were going to share some of it too. He knew all their little secrets, and it was time to expose them. If they believed they could just dump him and let him rot in prison, they were wrong.

He'd already given them too many chances to make amends. Once the NCAA got wind of the illegal perks he had provided, they'd be singing a different tune. He had enough fodder to write a book about it.

Those players owed him for everything. He opened doors for them, got them in front of the coaches, got them signed to lucrative contracts. Without him, they would have been nothing, or close to it. Where was their sense of fair play? Didn't they have a conscience?

The Scheme

Nevin Shapiro's life had been so very different just a few years earlier, when he hobnobbed with Miami Heat players and played booster to the University of Miami Hurricanes. He spent thousands all over Miami, everywhere from high-end restaurants to VIP rooms in strip clubs. He had wagered hundreds of thousands gambling and even shelled out $400,000 on Miami Heat floor seats.

So where did he find all that money?

On the face of it, Nevin Shapiro's Capitol Investment USA, Inc. sounded like a great investment opportunity. Investors provided the capital for Shapiro's grocery diverting business and profited with a 10%-26% annual return. The business grew rapidly.

Shapiro characterized Capitol as an arbitrage business. Arbitrage is the practice of taking advantage of price differences between two markets and earning a profit. Capitol bought groceries cheaply in one part of the U.S., then shipped them to a region where prices were higher. Capitol claimed it bought groceries from other wholesalers and diverted, or sold, the goods to more expensive markets.

The return was generous, and at first glance, the concept seemed plausible. Grocery wholesalers average around 15%-20% in annual profits. However, investors who dug a little deeper might have come up with some troubling questions.

The most blatant red flag concerned the wholesalers from which Capitol bought the goods. Why wouldn't these companies have "diverted" the goods themselves? Wholesalers and distributors typically have extensive, cost-effective logistics networks. If there were significant profit to be made in diverting goods, surely these companies would have investigated this alternative. In addition, many groceries are perishable, leaving little time to seek other buyers.

Capitol would also have to make a profit above and beyond what it paid investors in order to remain a viable business. How could it earn the average wholesalers' rate of return of 15%-20% even after paying investors 10%-26% to finance the inventory purchases? While not impossible, it is highly improbable. Let's look at the range of possibilities using an ending sale price of $100.

Ponzi #8—Nevin Shapiro

Working backwards from top to bottom, we find:

	Low	High
Final Sale Price	$100	$100
Capitol markup using grocery whole-saler average margin of 15%-20%	$15	$20
Capitol's Cost of Goods	$85	$80
(Included in cost of goods-interest to investors at 10%-26%)	$8.50	$20.80
Net-assumes this was original wholesaler's selling price	$76.50	$59.50
First wholesaler's markup of 15%-20%	$9.98	$12.28
First wholesaler's cost (assum-ing 15%-20% markup)	$66.52	$47.22

Does Capitol possess secret information enabling it to sell a $47.22 product for $100? Why doesn't the first wholesaler know this secret?

Obviously, there are ranges of pricing combinations, but the above example shows the range from low to high. For simplicity's sake, I have ignored other variables such as incremental transportation costs, since these would be similar under every scenario.

Now we will look at Capitol's value-added component of the grocery diverting business. It merely re-ships the goods to a new location. Capitol is not modifying the goods in any way, so the customer is not getting a better product.

However, Capitol's part in the supply chain adds an additional $23.50 to $40.80 to the final price, representing Capitol's markup of $15-$20, plus the financing cost of $8.50 to $20.80 it pays to the investors. That equates to a whopping 35%-

86% markup over the original wholesaler's cost. Put another way, that wholesaler could keep those goods and resell them for a 35%-86% profit margin, instead of the standard 15%-20%.

Wouldn't it make more sense for the first wholesaler to sell the goods themselves? In fact, they have a compelling reason to shift from their existing sales regions and open entirely new sales territories!

In the unlikely event that the original wholesalers did not resell the goods themselves, you can bet their competitors would come out of the woodwork to earn two to four times the industry norm in profits.

Maybe the first wholesaler sold the inventory to Capitol below cost or at less than the usual margins? Possible, but unlikely. Most grocery wholesalers would have at the least a regional network, if not a national one. Fuel and handling are significant costs, so they would probably sell it within their own network at a fire sale price rather than to an outsider. If the economies of scale do not work for the original wholesaler to ship beyond their region, they certainly will not work for a second company buying the goods with the original wholesaler's 15%-20% markup.

If it seems too good to be true, it usually is.

Based on the range of returns, you can see that even if the original distributor sold the groceries at fire sale prices, that distributor would still earn more on the groceries than by selling it to Capitol. Capitol's middleman arrangement doesn't add up.

Shapiro's grocery diverting business defies logic when you study the numbers. Too bad so many people did not perform the due diligence.

If the cost analysis doesn't convince you, consider

the rates the investors earned. From 2005 to 2009, the US prime rate ranged from 5% in 2005 to just over 3% in 2009, with a peak of 8% in 2007 before declining. As the prime rate declined, so did interest rates on loans. Why didn't Capitol obtain a bank loan at a lower rate?

Many banks would have been happy to provide favorable lending terms to a growing business like Capitol, especially with the grocery inventory as collateral. Of course we know now that there were no groceries, and hence, no collateral.

As you can see, demanding answers to a few simple questions would have exposed the scheme. A little analysis of publicly known information can uncover a wealth of interesting (and often conflicting) information.

Modus Operandi

Most frauds of any magnitude require the cooperation or collusion of several people. In Capitol's case, this included the CFO, Roberto Torres, accountant Alejandro Torres (Roberto's son), and an unnamed bookkeeper.

Shapiro and the others collectively misrepresented Capitol's financial status with doctored financial statements showing annual income averaging $50-60 million per year.

They also had to construct false invoices to convince investors of the buying and reselling of grocery inventory. They also concocted fictitious joint venture agreements with Capitol and other parties to create a false audit trail of non-existent transactions.

It worked for quite awhile, but like all Ponzi schemes, it had to collapse eventually. By January 2009, Capitol was unable to keep up with principal and interest payments to investors. Shapiro made various excuses, but by late November, several investors had had enough.

Sherwin Jerrol, a large investor in the fund, filed an involuntary bankruptcy petition against Capitol. It was then that investors' greatest fears were realized. Capitol was insolvent. It owed investors in excess of $100 million.

Worse, some of the investors had received preferential treatment, receiving their investment money back when they complained. Since a Ponzi scheme involves paying earlier investors with later investors, the disgruntled investors were really getting paid at the expense of other investors.

Where the Money Went

Shapiro diverted investor money for his own use, including $26,000 monthly mortgage payments on his Miami Beach house, and another $12,000 for payments on his yacht and Mercedes. The FBI estimates the total money he spent on personal items from 2005 to 2009 at $35 million, with $5 million of that used to settle gambling debts.

Like many Ponzi schemers, Shapiro used money to buy his way into exclusive circles. In his case, it was professional and elite athletes, including University of Miami basketball up-and-comers and NBA stars. He stroked his ego by rubbing shoulders with some of the highest-paid NBA stars. He donated $150,000 over ten years to the University of Miami, who in return agreed to name the student-athlete lounge after him.

After his arrest, his loyalties changed quickly. When the basketball stars steered clear of him, he threatened to publish a tell-all book about their exploits in violating NCAA rules. He named more than seventy University of Miami basketball and football athletes and alleged they had received millions in prohibited benefits—from him.

How It Ended

Like many of the Ponzi schemes in this book, a financial crisis sounded the death knell for Shapiro's game. New capital dried up in 2008, and by January 2009, Shapiro was unable to pay the promised returns. At first, he blamed late vendor payments. Later he used the lame excuse that his accountant was on vacation (accountants often shoulder the blame, guilty or not). When Sherwin Jerol forced involuntary bankruptcy in November 2009, Shapiro's fantasy world ground to a screeching halt.

In April 2010, Shapiro was charged with securities fraud and money laundering. He pled guilty in September 2010 and in June of the following year was sentenced to twenty years and ordered to pay restitution of $82.7 million.

The University of Miami removed all references to Nevin Shapiro and returned his earlier donation.

Once a Thief, Always a Thief

While many of these fraudsters gravitate towards

high-profile charity donations, they tend to otherwise help themselves rather than contribute to society as a whole. It is very unlikely they would be inclined to donate if they came by the money honestly. It is at odds with the very characteristics that drive them to steal and cheat in the first place.

A separate but related crime is that many (but not all) Ponzi schemers fail to declare their income and pay tax on it. Is it because in their minds it is not "real" money? Are they so brazen that they just assume they can get away with whatever they want and not pay their fair share?

Such was the case with one of Shapiro's agents, Sydney "Jack" Williams. Williams was an associate of Shapiro's and one of his primary sources of new investors into Capitol. In return for referring new investors, Williams received generous finder's fees of more than $12 million. Williams had also personally invested over $100 million in Capitol.

Williams was not complicit in Shapiro's fraud, and he did lose some of his investment. He wasn't completely on the straight and narrow, however. He attracted the attention of the Internal Revenue Service when they discovered that he had failed to disclose more than $6 million in income. That slip earned him a prison sentence, a fine, and a requirement to pay his outstanding tax bill.

Perhaps there is a simpler way to spot cheaters in general, in addition to Ponzi schemers specifically. If they cheat in one area of their life, their propensity to deceive in other areas is also high.

Rather than studying the investments they promote,

we should look at their behavior in other aspects of their lives. For instance, analyzing a taxpayer's ratio of tax paid in contrast to total charity donations might indicate undeclared income. The Internal Revenue Service could be the perfect place to uncover these fraudsters. They also have the authority to target them for a tax audit.

CHAPTER 8

PONZI #7—IOAN STOICA—
CHARITY BEGINS AT HOME

Ponzi Particulars	Ioan Stoica
Theme	Caritas Company, mutual aid scheme
Fraud	$1 Billion
Promised return	800x original investment in 6 months
Investors defrauded	4 Million
Date discovered	1994
Where	Romania
Prison sentence	18 months

Caritas Company, Cluj-Napoca, Romania, Fall 1993

IOAN STOICA OPENED HIS DOOR a crack and peered into the outer office. He felt a thump in his chest when he spotted the old man again, waiting about a half-dozen spots back from the front of the line. Stoica quickly moved to close the door but not before the grizzled old man locked eyes on him.

"You!" The man stepped out of line and rushed towards Stoica, never taking his eyes off him. "I want my money back. You're a thief!"

Stoica shook his head. "You will get your money back. But you have to follow the rules." He motioned to the line of people. "You have to wait your turn like everyone else."

"I have waited—my three months was up almost a month ago. I need to eat. Why are you being so difficult?"

Stoica dismissed him with a wave of his hand. "Just wait your turn." Without strict rules, his ruse would be quickly exposed. Every Romanian would be after him soon after that, since practically all of them had invested in his scheme.

The man swore under his breath but returned to the line.

Stoica turned his attention to the three clerks servicing the lines. They sat at a row of tables, stamping, stapling and counting money. Every single one was handing money back to customers, rather than the other way round. Money was running out. How could he turn this mess around?

Stoica caught the old man's eye again. He broke away from his gaze and refocused on the people at the front of the line. He had hoped some of them had come to deposit money because Caritas, his company, was in desperate need of cash. Deposits were unlikely—almost no one brought money in now. Dozens of people had slept outside this morning, waiting for the doors to open to withdraw their money, just like the old man. Desperation hung in the air as people fidgeted in the line.

He had suspended redemptions three weeks ago after running out of new money. Now he only allowed redemptions one day a month. But since the deposits had stopped, there wasn't enough money for even once a month. He would be lucky if the money lasted another hour.

A woman in a threadbare coat glared at him from the front of the line. A week ago, she would have flashed him a smile. She pointed behind her to where the old man leaned against his cane. "Why can't you give this old man his money?"

Stoica ignored her.

"Give me my money," the man raised his voice over the din of the crowd.

A rumble went through the people in line.

"You'll get your money," Stoica grumbled. "If you haven't already ruined it for everyone." He glanced warily at a half dozen men who had just stomped in from the cold. They took their places at the rear of the line. He could tell from their clothing that they were miners. They had returned to the city to claim their money. They would have pooled their money, scrambling to amass enough for a deposit of 200,000 lei or so. While that was only about $200 in hard U.S. currency, the sheer volume of people making similar deposits had made things very good for a while. Factory workers bought Mercedes and minks, unthinkable on the equivalent of a $60 a month salary.

He had even heard of a man who sold his only cow and sunk all his money in Caritas. The man's action wasn't as stupid as it sounded. If only these people knew what was good for them. He wished they hadn't pushed their luck and demanded their money back.

His thoughts returned to the miners, a militant bunch. They could be trouble, all together like that, especially after hours traveling on an unheated train. He'd better pay them and get them out of here, or things could quickly escalate out of control. After that, he was done with this scheme. He could disappear for a long time. If he ended things now, he still had enough left to live on for the rest of his life.

Ponzi #7—Ioan Stoica—Charity Begins At Home

He motioned to his assistant, who closed the doors behind the men.

Caritas

Caritas is the Latin word for charity, but in 1992 Romania, the only person getting a handout was Ioan Stoica. Stoica, a former bookkeeper at a chemical plant, was the mastermind behind the Caritas Ponzi Scheme.

Caritas holds a unique place in Ponzi scheme history. Never has an entire country been duped by a Ponzi scheme to the extent of the Romanian fraud. At one point, officials estimated that approximately one-fifth of the population, or four million people, had invested up to half of the country's total savings in the scheme. To understand how this could have happened, it is important to understand the political and economic climate at the time.

Less than two years had passed since dictator Nicolae Ceaușescu's regime was overthrown on Christmas Day, 1989. He and his wife were tried and convicted that same day, and later shot by firing squad. Romania abolished capital punishment less than two weeks later, on January 7, 1990.

Almost overnight, Romania changed. The Romanian Revolution of 1989 ended the Communist rule that had been in place since 1947. Ceaușescu was the last in the line of Communist leaders, having ruled Romania with an iron fist from December 1967 to December 25, 1989. For more than forty years, many Romanians had lived in poverty and repression.

The National Salvation Front formed the new

government and chose to bring about gradual reforms to transition the economy. Currency controls lifted, and the country began the transition to a free market economy. Despite gradual privatization and reforms, or perhaps because of them, Romania saw inflation of 60% in less than a year. The inflation, coupled with high unemployment and the austerity program mandated by the International Monetary Fund, pushed even more people into poverty.

It was into these bleak economic conditions that Ioan Stoica's Caritas Ponzi scheme was born in April 1992, barely two years after the revolution. Whatever hopes had been dashed after the revolution were temporarily restored by his promises of money to be made. People scrambled to find money to invest in Caritas right from the start.

Stoica soon had more money deposited with the company than he ever imagined. In mere months, he had gone from a bookkeeper's salary to piles of cash for practically no work at all. He opened a high-end store to further cash in on the free-spending winners as they bought luxury foodstuffs and clothing.

Stoica branded his scheme as a "mutual-aid" scheme. He promised an 800% return within six months. The idea was music to the ears of people who had endured almost two generations of poverty.

The returns seemed unbelievable, but to people with no firsthand experience with capitalism, his promise of riches sounded plausible. Given the country's annual inflation rate of 60%, incredible gains might just be possible, right?

Stoica ran a very effective marketing campaign by

publishing the weekly returns by person in the local newspaper. Stoica referred to them as "winners", further enhancing the carnival atmosphere. At its peak, the list was dozens of pages long. Thousands more arrived with cash daily, hoping to make money.

Soon people began flocking to Stoica's business in the city of Cluj-Napoca. Mayor Gheroghe Funar welcomed the activity and even provided space for Stoica's operation in the town hall. So much money was deposited that the Romanian government even had to print more banknotes. At one point, Caritas held approximately one-third of all Romanian banknotes in circulation.

But what exactly was the investment? It was somewhat vague. People knew only two things: they had to recruit their friends and relatives, and they wanted to be a "winner" like those people in the newspaper.

Despite the lack of underlying investments, Caritas attracted millions of investors who often lined up for hours just to deposit their life savings in the company. The winners' lists and word of mouth removed any doubt as early investors began to show their newfound wealth with new cars, washing machines, and real estate. Regardless of how it worked—it did work. There was tangible proof that people were getting rich.

Despite warnings from prominent bankers and economists, the government allowed the scheme to continue unchecked. No doubt, they feared another revolution if the people were plunged back into poverty again.

By late 1993, it was impossible to ignore the warning signs. Not only was it clear that there was no underlying investment, but the depositors began to dwindle. Many earlier investors decided to get out and stay out while they could, and the newer, poorer investors tended to deposit less. The newspaper's winners' list dropped down to only a few pages from almost fifty.

Stoica momentarily suspended operations and blamed a computer glitch. A second pause a few months later further fueled suspicion, until Caritas finally folded in May 1994. It was officially declared bankrupt in August 1994.

Stoica blamed the newspapers for causing Caritas' collapse and promised investors they would get their money back. Of course they never did.

Although Stoica was sentenced to seven years for fraud, it was reduced to eighteen months on appeal. His victims had no reprieve, however. Many had to work additional years to gain back the savings they had lost, or to repay the loans they had taken out. In the end, Stoica's victims received more of a prison sentence than he did.

CHAPTER 9

PONZI #6—A ROYAL RUSE - DAMARA BERTGES

Ponzi Particulars	Damara Bertges
Theme	European Kings Club, interest bearing "letters"
Fraud	$1.1 Billion US
Promised return	71%
Investors defrauded	94,000
Date discovered	1994
Where	Germany, Switzerland
Prison sentence	8 years

Gelnhausen, Germany—1992

THE BUZZ IN THE AIR was so strong it practically crackled. The packed room felt more like a religious revival than an investor meeting, and it energized Damara Bertges as she scanned the crowd. Hundreds of people squeezed into the rows of seats, all hoping for a chance to strike it rich. Some had been European Kings Club members for a few months or years, and some were new, hoping to get in on the action.

The crowd waited in anticipation and Bertges was not about to disappoint them. She loved this part—everyone happy. Money did that to people.

Each person bought the European Kings Club "letters" for the same price—1,400 marks—or 1,400 Swiss francs, if you were in Switzerland. Each EKC letter entitled the holder to 12 monthly payments of 200 German marks or Swiss francs each. It worked out to a 71% annual return on investment.

Irresistible.

Just as irresistible as the giant-sized cardboard checks and envelopes of cash she was about to hand out to carefully selected investors. The room buzzed with the energy of an American-style game show, with the "winners" designed to both incite the audience and bring in new money.

Lots of new money. There was no problem paying such attractive returns, as long as the European Kings Club continued to attract new investors to finance the payments. No need to look far, as a new batch of people arrived on her doorstep at every meeting. She could practically smell the money. Her only regret was not thinking of this idea sooner.

Swindled in Switzerland—the Scheme

The European Kings Club took place in the early 1990s in Germany and Switzerland, before the Euro was adopted as a common currency. Naturally, EKC's 71% return was guaranteed, given it was a Ponzi scheme. The scheme worked for several years. For a brief period, one in every ten people in certain Swiss cantons was an EKC investor.

The EKC was run by Damara Bertges, a charismatic German housewife from a modest background, and Hans Günther Spachtholz, a German doctor. The EKC, like so many Ponzi schemes, was an affinity fraud. A fraudster targets similar people as a group, often based on nationality, religion or ethnic background.

People tend to trust people like themselves, people they can identify with. This is particularly effective in religious groups, as people tend to assume that religious people are honest people. If a particular group doesn't exist, a clever scam artist can create one. In this case, it was a group of "little guys", supposedly exploited by the banks.

Not only did the "non-profit" EKC offer a higher return, it also allowed the "little guys" to avenge their supposed mistreatment by the big banks. At the very least, investing with EKC meant the "little guy" could stick it to the big banks and at the same time earn a spectacular return on an investment.

There was another twist to the affinity angle. European Kings Club's arsenal included something even more effective—a conspiracy theory or *konspirationistchen*. This theme pushed the idea that the big European banks, the European Community, and somehow the Masons all exploited the "little guy" as they actively conspired to steal from regular working people. Criminals often deflect suspicion from themselves by casting it on others.

The conspiracy theory also instilled strong feelings of patriotism and justice among EKC members. Even when returns dropped to 40% shortly before the collapse, they believed in their cause. It also helped that each existing member received a 10% commission for referring new investors. They were truly in this thing together. They even had their own song.

Affinity often overlaps with an exclusivity theme, and this was the case with EKC. Ponzi schemers play upon human nature by restricting the investment to a particular group. When something is offered to your group and not others, you feel fortunate—and special—to be included. It's like a gift.

You are less likely to question anyone who appears to be doing you a favor. You might also want to reciprocate by helping that person. Recruiting new investors fits the bill. It is exactly what the fraudster is looking for. In this type of closed environment, news spreads like wildfire, especially when it is a moneymaking opportunity. The fraudster doesn't have to advertise, which reduces risk of outside detection. The affinity and exclusivity themes allow the fraudster to control who is invited—and ensure authorities are kept in the dark.

Exclusivity also creates buzz and excitement, since everyone loves to brag about important connections or success. People also like to pass on great opportunities to their friends and family.

The party didn't last long. In late 1994, after only three years, the scheme collapsed, more than a billion dollars evaporated, and Bertges and Spachtholz stood trial for the largest Ponzi scheme in German history.

Yet even with criminal charges, the beliefs of many EKC victims held fast. Many of them felt that Bertges herself was a victim, taken in by her charismatic smile and engaging personality. They cheered for her and brought red roses to court for her. Despite this show of support, both Bertges and Spachtholz were found guilty and received sentences of eight and five years respectively. Bertges ended up only serving 3.5 years, after credit for two years already served prior to trial.

CHAPTER 10

PONZI #5—SCOTT ROTHSTEIN

Ponzi Particulars	Scott Rothstein
Theme	Rothstein, Rosenfeldt and Adler, structured legal settlements
Fraud	$1.4 Billion US
Promised return	50%
Investors defrauded	250+
Date discovered	1994
Where	Fort Lauderdale, Florida
Prison sentence	50 years

Fort Lauderdale, Florida—October 2009

SCOTT ROTHSTEIN SCOOPED ELASTIC-BANDED BUNDLES of hundred dollar bills from his office safe and shoved them into his duffel bag until it strained at the seams. He glanced over at his office door. Closed and locked. He had arrived through his private entrance, so no one had seen him come in.

He exhaled and turned the cash bundles over in his hand, glad to have had the foresight to keep the money in his office safe. He had known this day would come, although it had arrived much sooner than he had hoped.

This might be the only cash he would see for a while. He crammed the last two bundles into the sides of his bulging duffel, then squeezed the sides together and zipped it closed. The cash was his backup plan, in case the authorities intercepted his $16-million wire transfer, or it somehow failed to go through. The backup plan was likely overkill, since only he knew the total extent of Rothstein, Rosenfeldt and Adler's financial picture.

While he was careful to share only partial details with anyone else involved, the whole scheme had accelerated to the point that even he could no longer piece together all of the parts. Everything had mushroomed out of control, and he could no longer keep track of what monies he had promised to which investor. He also couldn't move money or doctor the statements fast enough. More importantly, he was unable to pay out the investments as they came due, despite the hundreds of millions in deposits he had received in just the last few weeks.

He had to escape while escape was still possible.

Rothstein hefted the duffel in his hand. A million dollars weighed much less than he had expected. He had always hoarded a significant amount of cash in his office. Having it within reach was safer here than in any bank, where it could be frozen or seized. This was the first time he remembered actually counting it, however. Not that he ever worried much about anyone else taking the money. He always figured there would be more money coming in. He hadn't expected the investor money to dry up.

A million no longer seemed like much money to him. Hundreds of millions was more the norm, that is until today, when he was forced to leave all his other possessions behind.

He paused and glanced again at his closed office

door. It was still locked. Only he and his executive assistant, Marybeth Feiss, had a key to his inner office. He also kept a 24-hour guard outside. The guard was arranged courtesy of his friend, Fort Lauderdale Police Chief Frank Adderly, who supplied off-duty cops in a mutually beneficial arrangement. Rothstein received protection, and the cops earned a little moonlighting stipend.

The safe door clicked shut as he closed it for the last time. He scanned his office, wondering how long until they searched every inch of Rothstein, Rosenfeldt and Adler. Anything the authorities found on the premises would be seized as evidence, likely forfeited forever. He wished he could take it all with him.

Photographs lined the walls, showing him with the rich, famous, and politically connected in Fort Lauderdale. Would they consider him a friend or a foe once the truth came out?

He checked his watch, wishing he could take more timepieces from his sizeable watch collection. He felt a pang of sadness at leaving them behind in particular. He could always find more investors and start over, but the watches? Some were irreplaceable.

Still, time was of the essence, and he could buy more watches and friends where he was going. He rose and opened the nondescript door in his office wall that hid his private elevator.

Broward County Sheriff Al Lamberti's right-hand man, Lt. David Benjamin, waited to escort him to the airport, where a private jet stood by to whisk him away to Casablanca, Morocco. Though he did not know it yet, he would return less than two weeks later, on the same jet chartered from Blue Star Jets. Florida Governor Charlie Crist's wife's ex-husband owned the aviation company.

Rothstein had been in good with Governor Crist, even helping to blow out the candles on his birthday cake recently. Governor Crist was shortlisted to be John McCain's running mate, and Rothstein, Rosenfeldt and Adler had been a major contributor to the Crist campaign, as well as McCain's. Now Rothstein's carefully cultivated relationships would go up in smoke, just like the political favors he had hoped to curry.

He sighed as he stepped into the elevator. Another day and he might not make it out of the country. It was now or never. Upon arrival in Morocco, he would take a breather and plan his next move. The most important task was to wire more cash and then figure out what came next.

Morocco happened to be the only country that had no extradition treaties with either the U.S. or Israel. Rothstein had asked his firm's lawyers to research the very matter just weeks before, stating that the inquiry was for a very important client who could soon be charged with fraud, money laundering, and embezzlement. Morocco was the only country that fit the bill.

Sorry...Sort Of

Rothstein did not disappear forever—or even for very long. Shortly after his flight to Morocco, he emailed a despondent note, full of apologies. Was his remorse genuine? Or was it just another con game?

Maybe the authorities would simply go away if they thought he was dead. He could hide out in Morocco for a while, then start a new life with his millions. It seemed like the perfect exit strategy.

The note was dated October 31 and is commonly referred to as Rothstein's "suicide note." A few sentences said it all—or maybe nothing at all—depending on your interpretation of the words:

> *"Sorry for letting you all down. I am a fool. I thought I could fix it, but got trapped by my ego and refusal to fail, and now all I have accomplished is hurting the people I love. Please take care of yourselves and please protect Kimmie (Rothstein's wife). She knew nothing. Neither did she, nor any of you deserve what I did. I hope God allows me to see you on the other side. Love, Scott."*

Scott Rothstein signed all his emails and notes in the same sickly sweet way, whether a note to his family, law firm or business associates. Did he truly understand the meaning of the word in his salutation?

Aside from that, what was he implying about his wife? Protect wife Kim from what? If she knew nothing, why was he worried?

Many suspected that Scott Rothstein was running not only from the law but also from organized crime. Some of Rothstein's associates were reputed to have connections with Israeli organized crime and the Sicilian mafia. While unproven, there are some interesting facts to consider.

Rothstein claimed people were after him. Even

before his escape to Morocco, he stated his life was in danger. Was it a fabricated drama, like so many other parts of his life? Or was there a ring of truth to the allegations? Why did he have 24-hour security?

It is difficult to know whether to believe Rothstein's claims of mob involvement, or to dismiss them as another attempt to gain favor with the authorities. He was sparse on details. Did he help them launder money? Did they invest money in his Ponzi scheme? The exact arrangement, if any, remains a mystery.

His openness about admitting guilt for not only his Ponzi scheme, but also other transgressions, led some to suspect his motives for cooperation. Was the allusion to mob ties merely a ploy to reduce his fifty-year sentence?

Maybe, but then why does his name not show up on the Federal Bureau of Prisons Inmate Locator list? Some believe he cooperated with authorities in exchange for a plea deal. His hefty fifty-year sentence does not mean a thing if he is not serving it.

While he might or might not be in witness protection, it is highly unusual for a convicted felon to be missing from the inmate list. Many questions remain unanswered.

The Scheme

Scott Rothstein based his fraud on the concept of discounted law settlements. The litigant, his client, signed over their settlement proceeds, which were payable at a future date. In exchange, the client received an immediate discounted payment today.

Rothstein's modus operandi was to present

this client advance payment as a money-making opportunity to a potential investor. The investor contributed the discounted settlement amount, supposedly paid through Rothstein's firm, Rothstein, Rosenfeldt & Adler (RRA), to his client, the victim. The investor then waited for the litigation outcome, and received the full settlement proceeds once the case concluded. The difference between the amount the investor paid up front, and what he later received represented profit to the investor.

How could Rothstein be so certain of a settlement amount for a case not yet decided? To overcome any investor objections, he added a twist. He claimed he could guarantee the investor's ultimate payout because of the nature of the suit.

Rothstein specialized in sexual harassment and workplace discrimination suits. He claimed to investors that many of the opposing parties to his clients' suits were willing to settle out of court, in exchange for confidentiality. Rothstein would propose a settlement, also mentioning the alternative of deposing the man's wife, children or his girlfriend. He alluded to embarrassing video footage to up the ante. He implied that everyone chose the former, loath to having their wife or girlfriend discover their secret life. Further, they never argued about the final settlement amount Rothstein suggested.

Rothstein added additional color to the stories, painting them as cases where the boss had slept with his secretary or had been caught with prostitutes. He even claimed to have video footage of the transgressions, which he threatened to disclose if the person did not agree to the settlement terms.

Coincidentally, many victims (his clients) wanted immediate payment, rather than wait for the full proceeds of their settlement later. It was all according to the confidential settlement terms Rothstein, Rosenfeldt and Adler (RRA) had apparently worked out with the other party to the lawsuit.

Investors were advised that confidentiality was mandatory for them as well, since it was part of the settlement terms. Surprisingly, investors never thought twice about the ethics of using what amounted to blackmail for the legal settlements. Did they ever wonder about the integrity of the man they entrusted with their money?

Rothstein took the investor checks and in return handed back a series of post-dated checks that matched the supposed cash flow and timing of the plaintiff's settlement. The investor then cashed the checks when the date on the check arrived.

It seemed like a perfect investment, given it was 100% guaranteed. Settlement proceeds were held in escrow, evidenced by the doctored bank statements Rothstein provided to his potential investors.

It was the perfect arrangement for Rothstein, too. He provided what seemed like a very plausible reason for secrecy, which helped him perpetuate his Ponzi scheme.

What was unclear was why Rothstein's clients would be willing to accept such significant discounts on their settlements. Rothstein's returns ranged from 20% to 45% or more. He seemed to have the ability to adjust those returns too. Any hesitation on an investor's part and the term length of the investment might decrease, or the percentage return could increase. Never mind the fact that these amounted to securities he was not registered or qualified to sell under federal law.

Aside from the too good to be true investment returns, no one questioned the blatant conflict of interest connected with selling his clients' settlements to his business associates. Nor did investors question what seemed to be blackmail or entrapment, since he implied that he often supplied hookers to place the men in compromising positions in the first place. Perhaps in their greed to earn a fantastic return, investors turned a blind eye.

While secrecy is a fraud red flag, Rothstein's reason for confidentiality seemed reasonable—at least on the surface. Given the size of Rothstein's firm with almost a hundred lawyers, it also was not surprising they had so many of these suits to settle discreetly. It seemed to be the perfect arrangement.

The 100% secure investment promised the investor was also a red flag. As Rothstein described in his deposition, the money was already supposedly "in-house" in an escrow account at RRA. That alone should have given prospective investors pause. If Rothstein's clients needed immediate cash, why couldn't they simply visit the bank for a loan, using the escrow money as collateral? Investors did not question this, seduced as they were by the promise of generous returns.

Rothstein and his helpers doctored bank statements to show inflated amounts of cash. They even went so far as to meet investors in the bank itself, in order to give the illusion of an independent third party. Rothstein would have an accomplice impersonate a bank employee and verify the bank balances on the statements.

A Web of Deceit

While Rothstein claims to have started his Ponzi in 2005, his deceit probably stretched back years prior, after he had won an employment discrimination settlement for a drug addict. He collected the money but neglected to tell or pay the addict. When she finally discovered she was owed money, he provided her with cash to fuel her drug habit. It formed the seed of an idea for the Ponzi scheme he would hatch years later.

Everything about Rothstein was a lie—or at least a contradiction. His grandmother scraped together money for him to attend law school, yet he was anything but frugal. Perhaps Scott Rothstein's persona and his ultimate downfall are encapsulated in his own words: "I grew up poor. I'm a lunatic about money."

After finishing law school, he practiced in relative obscurity for about fifteen years. Then he began a meteoric rise to the very pinnacle of Fort Lauderdale's legal community. By the time he joined up with partners Rosenfeldt and Adler, he lived larger than life, with matching his and hers gold toilet seat covers in one of his many homes, luxury sports cars, and motorcycles in the garage. Like Madoff, he had a yen for expensive watches, sporting a collection that was valued in the millions.

He considered himself a devout Jew, yet paid

thousands to an escort service and kept a stripper in a hotel room. Like many Ponzi schemers, he was driven by his ego and desire to connect with Florida's most wealthy and powerful. He exuded charm and charisma. Most investors took his spiels at face value, even though the paperwork to back up the investment details was lacking.

Rothstein was indiscriminate in who he swindled. Some of his biggest investors were Shimon and Ovadia (Ovi) Levy, a father and son who were his partners in The Sea Club Ocean Resort and the Renato Watch Company respectively. He considered Ovi and Shimon friends and family, or at least that was what he said to them. When they expressed an interest in his scheme, he did not hesitate to take their money. When asked about how he structured their deal at his deposition he said:

"In discussing the deals and the deal flow with Shimon and Ovadia, it became clear to me that they wanted very, very short payout deals, meaning over as few months as possible, to recoup their entire principal and their return on investment; so when I was structuring the deals for them obviously, you know, I was making them up."

When making up the fictitious deals, he also considered the cash needed to perpetuate the Ponzi scheme (getting critical at this point) in addition to the Levys' desire for a quick payout. He said he was also "trying to tweak the deals a little bit because they were very close to me and I wanted them to make a lot of money."

Some might find it ironic that while considering the

Levys as "family," he still took their money for a non-existent investment. Such is the self-rationalization of a fraudster.

At one point Shimon Levy even asked Rothstein point-blank if he was running a Ponzi scheme. He seemed to take Rothstein at his word when he replied "no" and did not investigate further. Despite the promised high returns with no risk over a very short time horizon, Levy ignored his earlier doubts and continued to roll his money over with Rothstein.

Renato Watch Company

Ovi Levy, his Renato Watch Company partner, requested and received police protection around the time Rothstein escaped to Morocco. A uniformed police officer stayed outside his gated community home from dusk till dawn for at least a week. Were his fears somehow related to Rothstein's disappearance?

Shimon Levy's former partner at the Sea Club Ocean Resort Hotel had been gunned down in broad daylight several years before.

Rothstein Returns

Shortly after Rothstein's late October flight to Morocco, he was somehow convinced to return voluntarily to the U.S. He admitted not only to his Ponzi scheme but also to what he called a "sub-Ponzi." In his deposition, he admitted to a multitude of crimes including securities fraud, money laundering, and tax evasion.

He seemed almost too eager to volunteer information. So far, he has been the most cooperative Ponzi schemer in history—even volunteering information about other criminal activities in addition to the Ponzi scheme.

What does he know, and whom does he know it about?

Money and Democracy

Scott Rothstein collected his friends in high places the same way he collected watches, cars and other luxury items. He tapped into the social circles of the well-connected as a way to get the inside track on lucrative contingency fee arrangements as well as expand his circle of wealthy investors to feed his Ponzi scheme.

Despite Rothstein's busy life, he also managed to find time to involve himself in politics. Like everything else, he immersed himself in the political arena in a big way.

Once Rothstein's Ponzi was exposed, authorities soon discovered other separate but related frauds were in play. The Ponzi scheme was simply the tip of a very big iceberg.

For instance, Rothstein sought to curry favor with political bigwigs. He felt he could to raise the political stature of RRA by making heavy contributions to the political campaign of John McCain. It was not the first time he had tried to cozy up to powerful political figures.

As with everything else, Rothstein first tried to figure out what people wanted, then found a way to give it to them. In his mind, they then owed him a favor.

But he couldn't simply write a big check. To skirt the requirements of the Federal Election Campaign Act, he needed many smaller contributions from RRA employees. That was problematic since many lacked either the means or the desire to contribute to the Republican's campaign. As always, Rothstein found a way around this problem.

A Fraud-Within-a-Fraud

Steven Lippman, an RRA lawyer, and other employees made individual campaign contributions, only to get reimbursed from RRA for the entire amount with a slight bonus. In Lippman's case, he contributed $67,800 but received an RRA reimbursement check for $77,500 for his troubles. The RRA check was backdated six days prior to the campaign contribution, with the check stub description reading "bonus."

Rothstein's assistant, Marybeth Feiss, issued the checks to Lippman and other Rothstein employees. The expenses were described in the accounting books as bonuses or expense reimbursements. The employee got his or her money back, and Rothstein gained favor with politicians by providing generous contributions that sidestepped the contribution limit laws.

Was it the first time he had tried such a scheme? Probably not, since fraudsters usually test the waters with smaller transactions first. His political contributions should also make you wonder how prevalent this practice is with other political contributions and what it means for our society. Today's campaigns require billions of dollars in financing. Who exactly are the politicians beholden to—voters or the financiers?

Lippman's loyalty to Rothstein seemed to have no bounds. As RRA's cash position worsened, Lippman engaged in check kiting to cover the fact that there was insufficient money in the bank to cover expenditures. Check kiting involves writing a check, knowing there are insufficient funds in the bank account to cover it. A check from a second bank is then immediately written, and deposited in the first account to offset the first check. This ruse takes advantage of the "float", which is the number of days it takes for the bank to verify the funds and clear checks between banks.

From February 2006 to February 2008, Lippman used an account he had kept active from his previous law firm (LVS), where he had been a partner. He wrote checks from the LVS account to overstate and misrepresent the RRA balances. The artificially inflated bank balance then allowed Rothstein to obtain bank financing for RRA that otherwise would not have been approved.

Lippman also wrote checks to LVS from the RRA account. High transaction volume gave the illusion of a busy successful law firm, but the money was simply moving back and forth between the two accounts. This practice capitalized on the two to three days normally required for checks to clear. The check showed as a deposit in the LVS bank balance, but it was still technically part of the RRA account, since it had not yet cleared the bank account. The money was effectively counted in two places at once.

From February 2006 to February 2008, Lippman issued $10.3 million in checks from the LVS account. During the same time, he issued checks totaling

$10.6 million from the RRA account—a net difference of only $300,000 as of the fraud discovery date. Since Lippman had access to both accounts, he controlled whether and when the checks were cashed, maintaining the façade of success.

Finally, Lippman submitted business expenses that were in reality his personal living expenses. Since these payments were classified as expense reimbursements, this provided RRA with a tax deduction and Lippman with tax-free payments. Lippman fraudulently avoided income tax on what should have been taxed as his income.

Lippman ultimately got a three-year sentence for conspiracy to violate the Federal Election Campaign Act, to defraud the United States, and to defraud a financial institution. But Lippman wasn't the only one running illegal schemes at RRA.

Yet Another Ponzi

Scott Rothstein's Ponzi scheme had all the elements of a Hollywood movie. Every rock overturned unearthed a new scheme. There was Rothstein's Ponzi scheme—the assigned settlements from which investors supposedly earned outsized returns. But there were many other frauds within RRA's walls, and outside of them too. Every new layer of deceit made it harder and harder to reconcile the details. When Rothstein needed more and more cash from new investors to keep his Ponzi alive, another fraud was born. Rothstein referred to it as a sub-Ponzi.

George Levin and Frank Preve

Fort Lauderdale hedge fund managers George Levin and Frank Preve operated Banyan Income Fund, through which they invested in Rothstein's "settlements." Within two years, they had allegedly defrauded 173 investors out of $157 million.

Levin and Preve purchased promissory notes from Rothstein for Levin's company, Banyan 1030-32, LLC, a feeder fund into Rothstein's Ponzi and its biggest contributor. When Rothstein's fund collapsed, theirs soon followed suit.

From July 2008 until October 2009, Preve and Levin sold promissory notes to investors through Banyan Income Fund, promising a fixed return ranging from 12% to 30%. They made a profit on the spread between the so-called return received on the structured settlements from Rothstein and the return promised to their investors.

Their offering memorandum described the fund's investment strategy as a continuation of one they had employed over the last two-and-a-half years, contributing over $1 billion into Rothstein's structured settlements. However, they neglected to add that half of that amount was late and still outstanding. Furthermore, they knew that Rothstein's ability to pay them rested on his capacity to obtain fresh capital.

Deals between Rothstein and Banyan often lacked paperwork. The SEC case alleged that Preve was fully aware that Rothstein's fund was a scam. They based their assumption on many emails between the two, including this one from Preve:

July 2008

"Missing documents....these won't go away so someone needs to do them...........you are also holding up our audit because I can't show anyone that I am a complete idiot by sending out millions of dollars with nothing to show for it except some e-mails that say 'Hey, Guido, send me 5 Mill.........I have such a deal for you.'"[2]

Rothstein indicated to them that he needed $100 million in order to resume payments. Based on this, Levin and Preve did exactly that, raising $100 million between May and October 2009, all the while knowing they were leading investors into a worthless investment simply to get their own money back. In the end, the $100 million was not enough. When Rothstein's Ponzi collapsed in October 2009, it took their contribution along with other investors' money.

Their Ponzi collapsed in conjunction with Rothstein's. They faced numerous securities violations, although several of those charges have been recently dropped.

The Aftermath

Rothstein's full cooperation meant forfeiting not only all his ill-gotten gains, but also losing all the assets he had purchased with the money. The list included almost too many cars to mention, including a Lamborghini, Ferrari, Maserati, Bugatti, Bentley, Corvette, Mercedes, Ford Expedition Limousine, Rolls Royce and a Cadillac Escalade. A couple of Harley

2   http://www.sec.gov/litigation/complaints/2012/comp-pr2012-100.pdf

Davidson motorcycles rounded out the list. Rothstein felt no need to narrow down his choices when he could buy with other people's money. He simply bought whatever he wanted without a second thought.

Rothstein's shopping sprees were not limited to cars. His 83-foot yacht, *Princess Kimberly*, was named after his wife. He also had a number of other boats, including a Sea-Ray, a Nor-Tech Super-Cat, a Riva Aquariva and a pair of Yamaha Wave runners. His prized watch collection was valued at over a million dollars, and his extensive real estate included waterfront homes. It was easy to see why the cash ran out.

His wife Kim, an ex-realtor and more than a dozen years Rothstein's junior, ostensibly helped surrender the assets, but she seemed to miss a few. Of course, there were simply so many assets, and it was difficult to keep track of things, especially with federal agents now swarming through her home.

Pretty much everything had been purchased with investor money, so there was practically nothing left for Kim. Kim and friend Stacie Wiesmann watched in horror as federal agents combed through the Rothstein house, seizing every item of value.

While they searched, Kim hid more than a million dollars worth of jewelry, including her 12-carat yellow diamond engagement ring, valued at $450,000. She gave the jewelry to Weismann and asked her to sell it for her. Kim still reeled from the shock of going from multi-millionaire to homeless in less than 24 hours. Selling the jewelry would give her something to live on while she figured out her next move.

Stacie attempted to sell Kimberly's 12-carat diamond ring to jeweler Sam Daoud, allegedly through Miami businessman Eddy Marin. She succeeded in selling some of the jewelry but then had a problem hiding the cash proceeds. She was not about to deposit the money in her own bank account. Further, even if the Rothstein bank accounts were not already frozen, Kim couldn't bank the money either. Kim then enlisted the help of lawyer Scott Saidel, who deposited the money in his law firm trust account.

It wasn't long before authorities discovered the plot. Lawyer Scott Saidel was charged with conspiracy and disbarred when it was revealed that he helped Kimberly Rothstein hide the proceeds from the jewelry sales. In October 2013, he received a 3-year prison sentence.

The net of collateral damage from Rothstein's Ponzi was cast even wider. Sam Daoud and Eddy Marin were charged with obstruction of justice and perjury for their part in the attempt to divert and hide the Rothstein jewels. Both pleaded guilty just before their scheduled trial date of October 21, 2013. Each faces a possible prison sentence of up to twenty years, although their sentences will likely be lower.

Kim Rothstein pleaded guilty to a conspiracy charge. After several sentencing delays, she received an 18-month prison sentence on November 12, 2013. On the same date friend Stacie Weismann was sentenced to 3 months in prison, 9 months home arrest and 3 years of supervised release.

Just days before Kim's sentencing, she filed divorce papers, alleging Scott verbally and physically abused her. She claimed Scott forbade her to leave the house after 6 p.m., and when she did go out, it was only with a bodyguard in tow. She professed no knowledge whatsoever of Scott's finances or his Ponzi scheme. Kim also claimed it was Scott who instructed her, through coded letters from prison, to have someone she trusted sell the jewelry.

Zero Sum Game

It is hard to separate truth from fiction when dealing with a Ponzi scam artist. After all, deception is at the root of everything they do. While Scott Rothstein has and is apparently cooperating with authorities, we can be certain he is doing so for his own self-interest. While his confession included accusations against his associates, such assertions will need independent corroboration with other evidence.

Scott Rothstein's victims no doubt regret having crossed paths with him, but in the strangest twist ever, they might ultimately emerge as the luckiest Ponzi pawns ever. In a July 2013 liquidation plan approved by a south Florida judge, the bankruptcy trustee will return all of the investors' original contributions as part of a compromise worked out between the trustee and creditors. As unlucky as they were to be ensnared in the scheme, they are possibly the only Ponzi scheme victims in history to get 100% of their money back.

In addition to tracing and ensuring clawbacks from early investors who withdrew more money than they originally invested, the trustee was able to prevail against the U.S. government for the proceeds from forfeited assets.

While it is a major coup for investors to have all of their money returned, it does not erase the time and stress of litigation, or investment income they could have earned while their money was tied up, either while invested with Rothstein or during litigation. However, it is a dramatically better outcome than any other Ponzi scheme on record.

CHAPTER 11

PONZI #4—TOM PETTERS

Ponzi Particulars	Tom Petters
Theme	Petters Warehouse Direct, Petters Group Worldwide, reselling consumer electronics to big-box retailers
Fraud	$3.7 Billion US
Promised return	Minimum 11% per year
Investors defrauded	20,000
Date discovered	2008
Where	Minnetonka, Minnesota
Prison sentence	50 years

Minnetonka, Minnesota—September 2008

TOM PETTERS ALWAYS HAD A knack for telling people what they wanted to hear. He had learned long ago that people rarely checked up on his claims. If they did, fine. He always had an explanation ready—and fabricated documentation to back it up.

However, reeling in more investors was hardly his biggest problem right now. Deanna Coleman, Vice President of Operations at Petters Company, Inc., sat opposite him in his office. She had just told him she wanted to call it quits. She had been with him 15 years, practically since the start. He couldn't allow someone with her knowledge to just walk away.

"Deanna, just take a few days off." She wouldn't spill the beans. He knew her better than that. Still, it made no sense. She earned more than $300,000 per year, and her annual bonuses topped seven figures. No one gave up all that without a reason.

Silence.

"C'mon, Deanna." He reached across his desk to pat her hand.

Deanna snatched her hand away. She crossed her arms and sighed.

Odd. She would not even look at him.

"What do you mean—you don't want to work here anymore?" After fifteen years of easy money? He couldn't believe it. "A week, whatever. Take off to your place in Costa Rica, I don't care. Just pull yourself together."

Deanna just shook her head.

"All right then, Las Vegas. Put it on the company Amex. You'll see things differently after a nice little break." After all these years and all they had been through together, this was the worst he had seen her. Why would she leave the best thing that had ever happened to her? It made no sense.

Robert Dean, Petters' Chief Financial Officer, stood in the doorway, behind Deanna, listening.

"Tom, I told you, no. I can't do it." She still avoided his gaze, preferring to stare at the floor instead.

"What's got into you?"

Silence.

"Deanna, I can't help you unless you talk to me. What do you want? A raise? How much?" Since joining the company in 1993 as his first employee, Deanna had gone from office manager to vice president of a multi-billion dollar holding company with controlling interests in Polaroid and Sun Country Airlines. He didn't think she wanted more money, but what else could it be?

"I don't want money. I just want it all to stop. It's too big, and it's out of control." She pushed the papers across the desk to Petters.

"No it's not," Petters said. Deanna might not need money, but the company required more money in order to avoid financial ruin.

He pushed the purchase order back towards her. "Just add another zero. No one's going to question the dollar amount on a Costco purchase order."

"No—I can't do it anymore. You do it." She dropped her pen on the desk and crossed her arms.

He had to find out why Deanna was acting so strange, but first, he needed backup paperwork for the new promissory note prepared and sent to the investment fund manager at Lancelot, who in turn would wire the money in exchange for the note. They needed that money today. This PO and the rest of the backup documentation were all that stood in the way of getting that money.

"I'll take care of it." Robert grabbed the paper off the desk. "I can handle Deanna's stuff. I'll make the POs and invoices."

"Thanks Robert." Robert Dean White, as Petters' CFO, was the other person in Petters' inner circle he could count on, although he did not trust him to quite the same extent as Deanna. She was the only person he trusted completely. He needed her more, he realized, than she needed him. Especially now, with no new investments.

He couldn't pay many of the overdue promissory notes, and he didn't want to field any investor questions either. Deanna had always kept on top of that. He shifted his gaze to Robert. "Did you wire the money to Lancelot?"

It was part of his plan to get solvent again. Without funds to pay the overdue notes, he had come up with an alternative. When the Lancelot hedge fund wired new investor money to Petters Company, Inc. (PCI), PCI immediately sent back the same money to Lancelot, but stated it was for repayment of several of the overdue notes. The repayment would include the original principal plus enough additional to equal the promised interest return.

Lancelot's manager was in on it. His investment management fees were based on total investments, and without new money, he wouldn't get paid at all. This round trip transaction was getting complicated, but Robert seemed confident about it.

Robert nodded. "Four of the five invoices. They want me to pay the fifth one tomorrow." Lancelot was a hedge fund and their primary source of investor money.

Petters' brow creased. "Tomorrow's too late. We need that money now."

"Relax. It makes sense. We can't have our outgoing wires in the exact same amount as what they wired us. It looks too obvious."

"Okay, you've got a point there." Petters nodded in agreement.

Petters rose and tapped Deanna on the shoulder as he headed for the door. He had to get moving if he was to make his Las Vegas flight in less than two hours. "See? Everything's fine."

Deanna jerked away, like he had the plague or something. She was acting kind of scary. He turned to Robert, who handed him the doctored purchase order.

"Not bad." Petters traced his finger over the zeroes on the purchase order. "But add another zero. It's Costco after all."

Early Life

Long before becoming Minnesota's biggest Ponzi schemer, Petters had a knack for selling. Joel Alsaker, his boss in an electronics store, said of Petters: "He was so talented—you can't overstate that fact. He could talk your wallet right out of your pocket."

Petters applied his talents to his former boss, borrowing $7,900 from him but not paying it back. When Alsaker asked for the money, he feigned bankruptcy.

Alsaker didn't take no for an answer and followed up with legal action. Petters went so far as to call the courthouse to advise that the case was settled, so the court date should be cancelled. When that did not work, he failed to show up for the hearing. It was an early example of Petters working the system—turning everything to his advantage without conscience.

In another incident prior to the start of Petters Company, Inc. (PCI) in 1991, Petters doctored a FedEx waybill as "proof" he had couriered a late payment. While never convicted of fraud for the counterfeit waybill, he was still ordered to pay up.

The Scheme

Petters began selling overstock and closeout merchandise through Petters Warehouse Direct in 1995. The company originally operated out of several stores in Minnesota, selling consumer electronics. In 1998, Petters expanded to online sales through Red Tag Inc. By 2000, he had transitioned exclusively to online sales, through Redtagbiz.com, a partnership with Fingerhut Companies Inc., a direct mail order company.

Petters raised capital to finance merchandise purchases by issuing promissory notes to members of the public, stating that the proceeds from the note sales would be used for "purchase order inventory financing." He claimed the financing bridged the gap between the purchase date from the manufacturers, who demanded payment up front, and the payment received from the retailers 180 days later. The retailers did not pay until they took delivery of the goods. Petters claimed his company purchased electronics at a deep discount and then resold the goods to big-box retailers at a profit.

The promissory notes were very attractive to investors. They paid an annualized return of at least 11% and were seemingly risk-free. Each note was secured, with the underlying purchased merchandise as collateral. Petters provided documentation that included details on the merchandise purchased, copies of retailer purchase orders, and the funding request from Petters Co., the purchaser of the merchandise. Given that the retailer purchase orders were from "big-box" purchasers like Costco and Wal-Mart, it seemed a very safe investment.

No one bothered to ask why global retailers with world-class logistics, global purchasing power, and razor-thin margins would buy through a smaller intermediary like Petters, which added at least the 11% financing cost. Nor did they question why Petters was unable to establish credit with the manufacturer, a normal business arrangement. Further, Petters did not purchase the inventory directly from the manufacturer. Instead, it came from two companies with interesting names: Enchanted Family Buying Co. ("Enchanted") and Nationwide International Resources ("Nationwide").

Enchanted and Nationwide were sham companies, each set up for the sole purpose of routing the money through another so it appeared Petters was buying inventory. Michael Catain, who lived on a street named Enchanted Point, received funds into Enchanted and then returned the money to Petters after extracting a fee for his troubles. Larry Reynolds laundered money through Nationwide using the same process. It was a less than transparent arrangement.

Regardless, the investment return was attractive, so investors were happy and business blossomed. Soon Petters expanded internationally, selling his notes to hedge funds as well as private investors.

Lancelot Investors Fund was one of those funds, started by Gregory Bell through Lancelot Management in 2001. This arrangement was even better for Petters. Though he had to pay Bell a cut of the proceeds, it meant he could raise much more money without spending time finding new investors. It also eliminated the need to deal directly with individual investors.

Petters and Bell had met prior to 2001, when Bell worked for another hedge fund that had invested in the promissory notes. By August 2008, Petters and Bell had raised over $2.6 billion from thousands of investors, including individuals, retirement plans, corporations, and hedge funds. Bell earned commissions of almost $250 million on the transactions.

By all appearances, Petters was a successful businessman. He had operated his own company since 1988, and his wealth grew as he acquired other companies, including Fingerhut Direct in 2002, uBid in 2003, Polaroid Company in 2005, and finally Sun Country Airlines in 2006. He accomplished all this despite multiple fraud convictions dating back to 1989.

Bell soon became aware of Petters' fraud convictions. He kept this from his investors, since he had some skeletons of his own in the closet. His Lancelot Funds were unregistered with the Securities & Exchange Commission, and his ill-gotten gains were ultimately channeled to his ironically named Blue Sky Trust, based in the Cook Islands.

Blue Sky laws are U.S. state laws designed to protect the public from fraud. The name originated in the early 1900s, when laws were enacted to protect against fly-by-night promoters who promised "speculative schemes which have no more basis than so many feet of 'blue sky'." At that time, investors were often duped by fraudulent claims of oil and gold discoveries, and other get-rich-quick schemes. The state laws were precursors of federal securities laws and the Securities and Exchange Commission.

Modus Operandi

Although Petters started the scheme many years before meeting Bell, it really took off when Bell began funneling money to Petters from his Lancelot Funds. Between October 2002 and August 2008, his funds invested over $2.6 billion in Petters' promissory notes.

Bell's company, Lancelot Management, charged the Lancelot funds management fees for investment advisory services. This included both a management fee of 0.5% and a performance fee of 20%, calculated on "new investment profits." As Bell was the owner of Lancelot, this earned him a cool $245 million, despite the fact that his investment advisory services consisted of simply handing over almost all of the investment monies to Petters for his promissory notes. Bell also provided performance charts and monthly statements (doctored of course) to investors in the funds.

According to the terms of Bell's confidential information memoranda, Lancelot would provide money to a company called Thousand Lakes LLC, which in turn entered into contracts with the so-called "vendors," Enchanted and Nationwide. Adding Thousand Lakes as middleman made it appear as though the transactions were arms-length, since Thousand Lakes was apparently independent from Petters and his company. The set-up gave the appearance of good investor protection and financial integrity.

Lancelot then provided the funds to Petters Co. in return for a "pre-existing" and legally binding purchase order that Thousand Lakes had received from a retailer.

How it actually worked was that Bell would simply email Petters and ask if he had any deals (or notes) available that day. Petters provided the purchase order after the fact to match whatever amount of money was available.

Lancelot would then provide the paperwork, including the promissory note, and copies of the bill of sale from the vendors (Enchanted or Nationwide) and the retailers' purchase order. Lancelot paid the investor money to Thousand Lakes, so that Thousand Lakes could pay the vendors. The vendors then supposedly shipped the goods to the retailers.

Bell told investors that he employed controls to safeguard their cash, including the use of a lockbox. He claimed investor money was transferred directly to the vendors and repayments were received directly from the retailers. In essence, Thousand Lakes was that lockbox, and he assured investors that Petters did not handle the cash directly. Money was paid to Petters Co. from the lockbox only after the transaction was complete and payment in full had been received from the retailers.

Nothing was further from the truth. While Bell's investor money did flow through Thousand Lakes, the payments from retailers did not. They came directly from Petters Co., and Bell had no visibility into Petters' arrangements with the retailers. When Bell questioned Petters on this, he did not receive a satisfactory explanation. Nevertheless, he was not about to jeopardize his commissions because they were too lucrative. Bell soon skipped the extra steps and simply sent the Lancelot Funds money directly to Petters Co. This was in direct contravention of the representations made to Lancelot investors.

Even at the height of the financial crisis the scheme still worked, although cash was getting tight. Lancelot Funds continued to invest everything in Petters' scheme. Bell's investors contributed another $243 million in the eight months from January to August 2008.

While money continued to pour into Lancelot Funds and then flow to Petters, more money than ever was needed. Petters' increasing use of cash and payment of Bell's generous fees grew to such an extent that the Ponzi scheme was in danger of collapse.

Bell still represented to his investors that he had his lockbox in place, that he had confirmed deliveries to retailers, and that he had inspected the vendor's warehouses. It was a blatant lie. Not only had Bell discovered Petters' criminal past, but he also realized Petters was using the investor money to fund his purchase of Polaroid Corporation.

Bell provided $360 million from the Lancelot Funds to help Petters finance the Polaroid purchase. This was not part of the investment mandate given in the Lancelot Funds Confidential Information Memoranda or operating agreements, and he knew it.

Petters and Bell modified outstanding promissory

notes to hide the money paid and never disclosed the Polaroid financing to Lancelot investors. Bell knew that if he quit the scheme, he would lose the hundreds of millions of dollars in deferred fees owed him.

In December 2007, to avoid the collapse of the scheme, Petters and Bell agreed to extend every promissory note by 90 days, but they did not disclose this to investors. In spite of this, Petters still could not make the payments in February 2008, so Petters and Bell created fictitious transactions to indicate the notes had been repaid and were replaced with new notes of equal value. They created a fake audit trail by wiring money from Thousand Lakes, supposedly to purchase new notes. Immediately after (sometimes within 30 minutes), Petters would send a wire for the exact same amount, supposedly to pay the overdue notes. Supporting documentation, such as non-existent inventory purchases and corresponding sales to the big-box retailers, was created for these round-trip transactions.

Petters and Bell executed hundreds of millions of dollars worth of these supposed repayments, later splitting the Petters repayment into two wire transfers a day apart so the round-trip transactions appeared less obvious. In the six months prior to the collapse of the Ponzi scheme, Bell and Petters did eighty-six of these round-trip transfers.

All of this activity created more complexity for the investor monthly statements, since these round-trip transactions had to be recorded somehow, with each note earning interest as well. Often investors would request details of the new notes, so Bell would fabricate spreadsheets with detailed accounting of the investments and interest payable.

It was becoming more difficult to track as the layers of fictitious transactions built upon one another. Bell became worried. From February to August 2008, he transferred much of his money out of his company into Swiss bank accounts.

Bell wasn't the only one. The flurry of activity was wearing on Petters' employees as well, many of whom had been with him from the beginning.

The Whistleblower

Deanna Coleman started with Petters in March 1993 and was Petters' longest serving employee. She eventually blew the whistle and later testified that the whole thing was a sham right from the start. Petters himself even referred to it as a Ponzi scheme behind closed doors.

One of her main duties was to fabricate invoices payable to the two phantom companies. The fake invoices provided a false audit trail to divert attention from the real outflows of money. Rather than paying nonexistent suppliers, the cash actually went directly into the pockets of Petters and his associates, or when necessary, paid off earlier investors.

Petters would create a fake purchase order for say, $1.5 million. An investor would not hesitate to invest $1 million, especially since PCI's cash receivable from a well-known customer like Costco more than covered his promissory note. PCI would pay the investor interest on his note, and the rest was supposedly profit.

There were so many troubling signs, if only investors had bothered to look. Several would-be investors who performed the due diligence discovered a trail of deceit and disgruntled former associates. One learned that Petters had lied about his education on a Dun & Bradstreet questionnaire. Despite only completing one semester at St. Cloud State University, he claimed a degree. Another investor called a PCI customer for independent verification of the purchase orders and discovered they were fake. Unfortunately, the would-be investor did not alert authorities, leaving the fraud to carry on unchecked until Deanna Coleman ultimately blew the whistle and turned herself in.

Even people wary of Petters' charms were eventually taken in. He was generous to a fault—with what we now know was other people's money. He threw elaborate parties and displayed all the trappings of wealth. He kept or owned at least five residences and drove a Bentley, and his monthly living expenses exceeded $200,000 per month. He had also used the investors' money for his corporate acquisitions, acquiring Polaroid and a majority stake in Sun Country Airlines.

Aside from Petters' luxury purchases, he had something else in common with many Ponzi scam artists: he made large charitable donations. He appeared to be a generous benefactor and philanthropist. His generosity—with other people's money—knew no bounds.

He donated primarily to universities and colleges. He donated $10 million to the University of Miami, $12 million to Rollins College, and $2 million to

Saint John's Abbey at Saint John's University. A $5.3 million donation to the College of St. Benedict got his name added to the Thomas J. Petters Center for Global Education. He also formed the John T. Petters Foundation, named after his late son, killed in Italy after trespassing on private property.

The sizable donations stolen from investor money stroked his ego. Like many other Ponzi schemers, Petters liked to see his name immortalized. He might have also made the school donations as a way to overcome the shame he felt being a college dropout. Maybe he had something to prove to himself and others, and the donations were a way of showing off his success despite the lack of a college degree.

Finder's Fees

Integral to Petters' scheme was employing others to find new investors and capital for the business, similar to his arrangement with Bell. He had no shortage of these agents due to the generous commissions he paid, including $42 million to another associate, James Nathan Fry. Potential investors might as well have had targets on their backs.

Frank Elroy Vennes Jr. was also one of Petters' most active agents. Vennes, an ex-con, partnered with Fry to establish two hedge funds under the name Arrowhead Funds. Fry was the front man and Vennes operated behind the scenes. Potential investors were unlikely to invest with an ex-con with previous convictions for money laundering, firearms, and narcotics violations.[3]

3   FBI press release US Attorney's Office District of Minnesota, June 12, 2013

Potential investors were told that Arrowhead loaned money to Petters (PCI) to finance purchases of inventory, which was then resold to big-box stores. In return for the capital, PCI provided promissory notes to Arrowhead.

Meanwhile Petters and his associates' lifestyles became more and more extravagant. They drove fancy cars and took exotic vacations and Las Vegas gambling junkets all on the company dime. All the monetary rewards made it hard for Deanna Coleman to do the right thing, especially at first. She not only enjoyed the cars and vacations, she even had PCI pay her brother and her boyfriend $1.2 million to hide assets during her 2007 divorce.

Kiss and Tell

Most Ponzi schemes are uncovered when the money runs out. Petters' scheme was discovered sooner than it otherwise might have been when Deanna Coleman became a whistleblower. She exposed the fraud in September 2008 in return for a plea deal. In another twist, Coleman also happened to be Petters' ex-lover and a key part of the scheme.

Coleman wore a wire to obtain enough evidence to convict Petters, Bell, and the others. On one of the wire transfers, Petters tells Coleman "they each have their different levels of what they can take."

I suppose you could read that sentence two different ways.

Petters raised more than $4 billion through

2013http://www.fbi.gov/minneapolis/press-releases/2013/federal-jury-finds-mound-hedge-fund-manager-guilty-of-lying-to-investors-in-connection-with-investment-in-petters-co

Arrowhead, Lancelot, and other investment funds. The investor money deposited in these funds was again used to perpetuate Petters' fraud. He bought other legitimate companies such as PDC (a successor of Polaroid) and Sun Country Airlines with his ill-gotten gains.

His scheming knew no bounds. He even created fraudulent retail orders from the acquired companies, which he used to overstate their revenues and receivables. The exaggerated amounts enabled him to indebt the companies with large loans, which he repurposed for his own use.

Petters headed a large conglomerate that owned or controlled 60 companies with global operations and over three thousand employees. In 2007, the year prior to the Ponzi discovery, the consolidated annual earnings were $2.3 billion.

As a direct result of the Ponzi scheme, Sun Country Airlines went bankrupt, as did PDC. In addition to the ruined investors, many people lost their jobs.

CHAPTER 12

PONZI #3—ALLEN STANFORD

Ponzi Particulars	Robert Allen Stanford (Allen Stanford)
Theme	Stanford International Bank, certificates of deposit
Fraud	$7 Billion US
Promised return	Returns averaging 12% per year
Investors defrauded	50,000
Date discovered	2009
Where	Antigua & United States
Prison sentence	110 years

Houston, Texas—June 2012

ALLEN STANFORD WAS FURIOUS, ALTHOUGH he tried not to show it. Losing his temper would just get in the way of what he wanted and needed right now: sympathy. This was his moment of truth. Would his jail sentence be five years or thirty? Thirty was impossible, since he was already sixty-two years old. Judge Hittner was ten years older than him. He hoped that age might work in his favor for the sentencing.

But Judge Hittner was ex-army and an Eagle Scout; he did things by the book. His habit of sticking to strict guidelines did not bode well, Stanford thought, as he broke out in a sweat. On the other hand, he hadn't killed anybody. Losing a bit of money certainly didn't mean he deserved to die in prison.

Stanford mustered what he hoped was an ingratiating smile and fixated on the judge. He was careful not to smile too broadly, lest it come off as his trademark smirk. He was going for a look that was remorseful yet pleasant. Surely the judge would take all factors into account.

This trial was the epitome of injustice. He couldn't get decent legal representation, and his so-called crimes had been blown out of proportion. His bank had been real, not a sham like those other Ponzi schemes he was being compared to. Yet no one seemed to understand it.

Stanford could not do anything about the charges, as he had already been convicted on thirteen counts of conspiracy, wire and mail fraud. He had managed to delay his trial for more than three years, but the sentencing by only three months. He had hoped it would all blow over. He knew that the more time passed, the more lenient the sentence was likely to be. People might not forget, but some might die in the meantime, or at least move on with their lives.

It was impossible for him to carry on with his life, he thought, as he scanned the packed courtroom. Who were all these people? He turned his thoughts back to his potential sentence. As short a sentence as possible please, since he didn't intend on rotting in prison with a bunch of thugs. The prosecution had asked for the maximum, a completely ridiculous two-hundred and thirty years. No way could he handle that. Nor should he have to.

Prison conditions were simply deplorable. He could manage five, maybe ten years maximum. With a convincing enough performance, he knew he could knock years off, maybe even decades. Surely it was possible to whittle his sentence down to something more reasonable.

Why did people insist on calling him another Madoff? He was nothing like him. Unlike Madoff, he had invested in real assets, not fictitious ones. Until the government shut it down, he had a real bank. How could a legitimate bank be a Ponzi scheme? Depositors had invested their money in good faith, in real enterprises. His intentions were good, so how could that be a fraud?

He could have returned the depositors' money too, if the government hadn't stepped in with their panicked statements and Gestapo tactics that started the run on his bank in the first place. They should be the ones on trial.

Naturally, they escaped blame, and he paid the price for their ineptitude. Nobody at his sentencing hearing today even cared that an insane inmate had already beaten him within an inch of his life. Nor did they care about the possible brain damage inflicted by that savage. He could barely think straight. He had likened his brain to Swiss cheese after reading up on brain damage. He liked that analogy.

He had researched the anti-stress drugs the doctors had prescribed, too. Some of them caused some nasty side effects. He had more than paid for any unintentional transgressions. No one deserved to suffer the way he had these last few years. He was perhaps the biggest victim of this whole mess.

He had also fired half-a-dozen lawyers because

they were incompetent, lazy, or money hungry. He made a mental note of all the mistakes they had made. That could also be grounds for an appeal.

Allen Stanford took in a deep breath and fixed the judge with his most convincing expression of integrity. "Stanford was a real brick-and-mortar financial institution. I am not a thief." He hoped his words rang with enough conviction. He had practiced in the mirror while he shaved and thought the words came across quite well. How could the judge not recognize this travesty of justice?

He studied the judge as he finished speaking. The judge's expression remained blank, other than motioning to an elderly woman who stood at the front of the line of a dozen or so people waiting to speak. Now he had to listen to a bunch of self-serving people cry about their ruined lives. They blew it all out of proportion in their victim impact statements. At least they could see the light of day. He, on the other hand, faced years inside a prison.

Even his employees had turned on him, trading testimony for lighter sentences. James Davis, his former university roommate and most recently Stanford Group Chief Financial Officer, had ultimately betrayed him the most, just to save his own skin. That was the thanks he got for handing him a great job and a life of luxury.

Meanwhile, his three years in prison so far felt more like thirty. Stanford snapped to attention as Judge Hittner began to speak. He locked eyes on the judge's mouth as he described the charges.

Stanford's pulse quickened and his face flushed.

The judge's negative tone was a bad sign. His knees buckled when he heard the sentence: one-hundred and ten years.

Trouble in Paradise

Stanford's lengthy sentence was likely influenced by Bernard Madoff's earlier Ponzi, which publicized the plight of the many victims. Federal sentencing guidelines also consider the extent of the loss, and Stanford's lack of remorse would have been a significant factor as well.

Before Robert Allen Stanford found himself with a century-plus sentence in Florida's high security Coleman Federal Correctional Complex, he was one of Antigua's most respected residents. Sir Allen was a billionaire banker, named Man of the Year in 2008 by World Finance magazine.

His life was idyllic. Sunny weather, the northeast trade winds, and cricket were constants of daily life in Antigua, where he based his operations of the Stanford Financial Group.

Since his arrival in 1998, he had entrenched himself in every aspect of Antiguan life. His bank was the island's largest employer after the Antiguan government. Stanford had his name on everything, from the rejuvenated cricket field to his Stanford International Bank. His funds built the hospital, and owned one of the largest private jet fleets worldwide.

He became an Antiguan citizen in 1999, after generous campaign contributions to the Prime Minister's re-election that year, and a $5 million interest-free loan to the government after Hurricane

George, a category 4, devastated the island.

He probably would have renamed the island Stanfordville if he could. But there was no need. Every single one of the island's 85,000 residents knew him by sight, and understood implicitly how important he was to their everyday existence.

Stanford was more than just important: he was vital to the local economy. His net worth of $2.2 billion was almost double Antigua's annual GDP of $1.2 billion. He spread his money around and his name along with it. He took care of things the government did not, or could not do, like revitalizing Airport Cricket Ground. He increased the seating capacity to five thousand, ensuring it was renamed Stanford Cricket Ground for his troubles.

Stanford also cut an imposing figure. At 6-foot-4 (193 cm), he towered over just about everyone. He could be intimidating, and he certainly was accustomed to getting what he wanted. Whether he reached his goals due to his stature, social standing, or ostentatious wealth didn't really matter to him.

Respect and power all came down to one thing: people judged you not on what you did, but on what you owned and controlled. Most important of all was what you could do for them.

Allen Stanford had always skated on the thin edge of the rules—and gotten away with it. Why shouldn't he? He deserved whatever wealth he could obtain. What was good for Stanford was good for Antigua. He had discovered early in life that people believed pretty much anything, provided you said it right. Especially when it was to their benefit to do so.

Ponzi #3—Allen Stanford

If there was money around, he could almost smell it. No matter how big the lie, it all worked the same. And if you were going to lie, you might as well go big.

Sir Allen

As Stanford's riches accumulated, he also set about reinventing himself. The Texan began wearing crested blazers, promoted cricket, and seemed to lose his Texan accent in favor of a vaguely British one.

In the fall of 2006, Stanford was awarded the title Knight Commander of the Order of the Nation (KCN) of Antigua and Barbuda. He immediately started calling himself "Sir Allen." His transformation from a Texan into British aristocracy appeared complete.

He claimed Queen Elizabeth II had knighted him, which was untrue. The only connection was that Prince Edward, the Queen's grandson, happened to be in attendance at the ceremony as part of Antigua's Silver Jubilee celebrations. Stanford's title was bestowed by the Antiguan government, not the Queen. As a pathological liar, he knew that hardly anyone would question him and fewer still would fact-check.

Soon after arriving on the island, Stanford set about cultivating an aristocratic image for himself. Whatever he lacked in Antiguan credentials, he soon made up for in other ways. To Stanford, respectability meant philanthropy and old money sports like cricket. In 2008, he organized a high-stakes winner-take-all cricket match between England and his own Antiguan team, the Stanford All Stars.

The match, designed to attract big-name teams and players, boasted high stakes unheard of in the cricket world. Winning the game would make each player on the winning team a millionaire.

The Stanford Cricket Ground, nicknamed the Sticky Wicket, hosted many 20/20 matches, including the Stanford 20/20. This was part of the Stanford Super Series, a week-long match with a $20-million purse to the winner of the final game.

On November 1, 2008, England was matched against the Stanford Superstars, the previous Stanford 20/20 winners from Trinidad and Tobago. The tournament received global media coverage, and cameras also picked up Stanford cavorting with the English players' wives and girlfriends in the stands while the game was underway. He pulled a cricketer's wife onto his lap just as the JumboTron cameras landed on them.

English player Matt Prior looked up from the field in shock to see his wife sitting on Stanford's lap. She felt powerless to act, worried about reacting while being filmed on the big screen. Stanford later apologized. There seemed to be no lasting repercussions, at least not for Stanford.

Stanford once again pushed things to the limit, just to see what he could get away with. As a billionaire, that was usually plenty. He simply did what he wanted, and if it didn't go over too well, he would beg forgiveness later.

Was he trying to throw the English team off their game? After all, $20-million was riding on it. In the end, the English team lost. Whether it was due to Stanford's shenanigans with the players' wives will never be known for sure.

Ponzi #3—Allen Stanford

Red Flags and Warning Signs

Stanford's checkered past foreshadowed trouble ahead. He was anything but transparent about his early years and preferred to keep details hidden. Stanford grew up in Texas and graduated with a finance degree from Baylor University in 1974. Soon after graduation, he started a chain of health clubs in Texas.

Unknown to Stanford International Bank depositors, Stanford had previously declared personal bankruptcy in 1982 after his Total Fitness Center health club chain also went bankrupt in Waco, Texas. His bankruptcy filing listed $13.6 million in liabilities and only $200,000 in assets. Perhaps the bankruptcy was why he had dropped his first name (Robert) and now simply called himself Allen Stanford.

In 1983, he packed his belongings from his rented house into his beat-up car and headed for greener pastures, skipping out on about $30,000 in unpaid rent. Stanford's landlord won a judgment against him in his first-known brush with the law.

Stanford then turned to real estate speculation in Houston, where he was reasonably successful. Soon after, he resurfaced on the Caribbean island of Montserrat, where he established the Guardian International Bank in 1986.

Montserrat was a known haven for drug cartel money and lax banking regulations. Even tiny Montserrat had issues with Stanford because he had tried to hide his bankrupt past. He did so because he was aware that regulatory authorities would quash his bank application. Charles John, the Financial Secretary of Montserrat, stated in a November 1990 letter to Stanford that he had failed to employ an approved auditor, and that the bank operated in a "manner detrimental to depositors." The letter also raised the fact that Stanford, as a former bankrupt individual, did not meet the requirements for a bank director.

As Montserrat tightened its regulatory grip on Stanford and revoked Guardian's bank license, Stanford simply relocated to the nation of Antigua & Barbuda. In 1991, he started a new bank with a new name: Stanford International Bank.

Stanford had other legal troubles. He had been charged with tax evasion on his 1990 US tax return. Americans are required to declare worldwide income on their US tax returns. Stanford did not. He and then-wife Susan underreported their joint 1990 income by more than $400,000.

All of these red flags went unnoticed or unheeded by investors and authorities. Stanford certainly did not volunteer information, and authorities either missed the signs, or turned a blind eye. Wealth often gives the owner a free pass from scrutiny. People rarely ask the rich and powerful the same questions they do of the lower classes.

Stanford's status as a major employer on the island, and the fact that his wealth exceeded Antigua's GDP, likely contributed to his preferential treatment.

Illusions of Grandeur

While the Stanford International Bank motto was *Hard work, Clear vision, Value for the client,*

Stanford's personal credo couldn't have been further from such ideals.

Instead of hard work, he spent his time socializing with the rich and famous, politicians in particular. He entertained on his fleet of yachts and flew friends around on his numerous aircraft.

Clear vision seemed to apply only to others. He was anything but transparent, as he secretly diverted millions of investor funds to support his lavish lifestyle.

Value for the client meant that anything of value seemed to end up in his pockets. The values he demanded of his employees did not appear to apply to him personally.

The truth remained hidden behind the illusion Stanford had created for himself. For the briefest of moments, he had the world in his hand. He was the sole shareholder of the Stanford Financial Group, with $50 billion in assets under management and a global presence in 140 countries. He was #205 on Forbes Richest Americans list, with an estimated fortune of $2.2 billion. He had all the trappings of wealth and was a dual U.S./Antigua citizen. Some even said he controlled the Antiguan government. At the very least, the Antiguan government was indebted to him, to the tune of $87 million. He appeared to be a generous benefactor, both on and off the island. He spent freely on revitalizing Antigua's public infrastructure.

Aside from fabricated financial results, Stanford spun other tales. He was especially interested in fabricating a past, one more respectable and pedigreed than his ordinary childhood in Texas.

Most notable was his claim that he was a descendant of Leland Stanford, founder of Stanford University. He underwrote the restoration of the Leland Stanford mansion in Sacramento, California, implying that the university founder was his relative. He stated that he wanted "to help to preserve an important piece of Stanford family history." The only problem was that it was not his family.

When a university spokesperson disputed the relationship, Stanford hired a genealogist to trace his roots. He insisted that he was a sixth cousin, twice removed. He did not stop until the university filed suit for trademark infringement.

He cultivated an image for Stanford International Bank as well, claiming its roots went back seventy-seven years earlier, when his grandfather Lodis Stanford had established his insurance business in tiny Mexia, Texas. In fact, the two companies were completely unrelated. However, it did not stop him from displaying an oil portrait of his grandfather at the bank's offices. He was all about image and respectability. If Stanford and his bank lacked these traits, he fabricated them.

He spent millions to enhance his image. In addition to cricket, he sponsored polo, tennis, and golf, and plastered the Stanford International Bank eagle logo everywhere, from his buildings right down to the crests and pins every Stanford employee wore.

Stanford's carefully cultivated image seemed bulletproof. However, before he perpetrated one of the biggest Ponzi schemes of all time, there were signs of his sociopathic personality.

Ponzi #3—Allen Stanford

He had a narcissistic craving for adulation and respect. While he did not stand out in his home state of Texas, he was a big man about town in Antigua.

Web of Deceit

"It was a classic case of the rat being put in charge of the cheese," Marian Althea Crick testified at Stanford's Houston trial. As Antigua's top banking regulator, Crick had plenty of expertise. She had suspected Stanford's criminal motives almost as soon as he started up Stanford International Bank (SIB) in Antigua in 1996. It had not escaped her attention that Stanford's arrival coincided with the crackdown in neighboring Montserrat, where he had been running Guardian International Bank.

Soon after Stanford's arrival on the island, his cozy relationship with Antigua's then-prime minister became apparent. Lester Bird, a lawyer by profession, had succeeded his father, Vere Bird, thereby cementing the Bird family dynasty by becoming Antigua's second prime minister since gaining independent rule from Britain. Lester Bird held the office from 1994 to 2004.

Crick's criticism referred to the fact that Bird had appointed Stanford to an advisory board seat of the regulatory agency that oversaw banking activity on the island. Like Crick's rat guarding the cheese analogy, Stanford's seat was a clearly a conflict of interest. The owner of a regulated bank should never have supervisory oversight over itself, or make the rules under which his own bank operated.

While Crick succeeded in having Stanford removed from his seat, he continued to meddle. Stanford used his influence to try to get her fired when she asked too many questions. When that didn't work, Stanford waited until Crick was away in 1998 to briefly take over the newly established Financial Services Regulatory Commission (FSRC). The Attorney General intervened when Crick complained, and Stanford was kicked out.

Ever tenacious, Stanford established an office of employees in 1999 to work on Antigua's regulatory banking reforms. In 2001, while Stanford International Bank was undergoing a regulatory audit, Stanford used his government influence to try to send Crick and the auditor examining SIB on a month-long international trip. His plan was to replace the auditor with a more agreeable one.

When his underhanded tactics failed, Stanford tried to curry favor with Crick by upgrading her economy air travel to first class. Crick reported Stanford's antics, but the government took no action. Crick eventually resigned in 2002, much to the delight of Stanford. Now he could operate with impunity.

Crick's replacement was Leroy King, a much more malleable and agreeable fellow. Stanford immediately began courting him, paying him millions in bribes, and providing him with private jet trips and NFL Super Bowl tickets to ensure his cooperation.

Stanford's tentacles now reached into the highest echelons of Antigua's government. He participated in writing the banking reform legislation under which his bank operated and he had King in his pocket. He used King to manage SIB's regulatory audits. King certified SIB's fictitious investment returns and financial position, thereby misleading investors, other regulators (such as the United States Securities and Exchange Commission (SEC)), and others. In essence, King claimed that SIB's investment portfolio had been verified.

Aside from King's rubber-stamped audits of SIB, he also provided Stanford with access to confidential regulatory information about Stanford and SIB, including details on inquiries from the SEC regarding Stanford. King was essentially a puppet, assuring the SEC there was no cause for concern. Perhaps even more shocking, Stanford drafted some of King's responses to the SEC information requests.

King was eventually implicated and charged in Stanford's Ponzi. As of this writing, he is awaiting extradition to the United States to stand trial. Marian Crick reassumed her position as Financial Services Regulatory Commission Chair in February 2009 when King was removed from his post.

The Crime

Allen Stanford operated a complex web of international companies. At the top was the Stanford Financial Group (SFG), of which Stanford was the sole shareholder. SFG in turn owned Stanford International Bank (SIB), a private, offshore bank, Stanford Group Company (SGC), Houston-based investment advisors, and Stanford Capital Management (SCM), which managed the investment portfolio.

Stanford International Bank sold $8 billion in high-yield certificates of deposits (CDs) through the network of financial advisors. The CDs were very popular for two reasons. They provided a lucrative return of 1% selling commission plus a 1% annual trailer commission to the financial advisors who sold them, and the rate of return for investors was greater than the deposit rates offered through a traditional bank.

These high returns did two things: they enticed investors and attracted the advisors with the largest books of business, who in turn would convert their clients' money into Stanford's CDs.

Traditional banks pay depositors a return in exchange for keeping their money on deposit with the bank. They then loan out this money at a higher rate, and earn their income on the spread between the interest they receive from borrowers and the interest they pay to depositors. Stanford's CDs were very different, since the investment proceeds were not loaned out. Instead, the money was invested on the clients' behalf.

While U.S. banks paid less than 3.2% for a three-year CD, SIB quoted a 5.375% fixed return. A five-year SIB CD earned more than 10% annually. How were they able to offer such outsized returns?

SIB claimed a "globally-diversified portfolio" of assets. These assets increased very quickly, averaging a growth of more than $1 billion per year. As of November 2008, SIB claimed $8.5 billion in total assets.

SIB stated that the exceptional returns it earned on its asset portfolio allowed it to pay higher interest rates to depositors. The money was supposedly invested in very liquid assets, which earned exceptional returns.

The problem? Most of the asset portfolio was known only to two people: Allen Stanford and his chief financial officer, James M. Davis.

Even co-conspirator Laura Pendergest-Holt, SIB and SFG's chief investment officer, was not privy to the supposed asset information. Pendergest-Holt headed a team of twenty-plus analysts who assisted her in supposedly overseeing the entire investment portfolio. However, Pendergest-Holt and her team only had access to the assets designated as the Tier 2 assets.

Within the company, the investment portfolio was segregated into three tiers. Tier 1 assets were cash and cash equivalents. Tier 2 was represented as investments with outside portfolio managers, and Tier 3 were assets managed by SIB itself. However, no SIB employees other than Allen Stanford and James Davis had access to the Tier 3 assets. Pendergest-Holt was the chief investment officer, yet she was not privy to the part of the investment portfolio that made up the bulk of the assets. As of December 2008, the Tier 3 mystery assets represented 81% of SIB's investment portfolio of $8.4 billion.

This 81% was further broken down into 58.6% equity, 7.2% precious metals, and 15.6% alternative investments. No further disclosure was provided, and no one seemed to ask—at first.

Stanford's liquidity problems began in 2008. The global financial crisis came first, but his issues compounded when news of Bernard Madoff's Ponzi scheme broke. When worried investors asked if Stanford might somehow take the money and run, they were assured he could not. Pendergest-Holt and her twenty analysts based in the U.S. were the supposed check and balance against this happening.

In December 2008, SIB also told investors that the bank had no exposure to Madoff's fraud. However, at the time they actually did have exposure. Approximately $400,000 was at risk through their investment in a Tremont Partners fund, Meridian, which in turn had invested with Madoff.

Pershing LLC, a clearing agent and custodian for Stanford's assets, also became alarmed due to a large number of wire transfers that had transferred money from client investment accounts to SIB. Between 2006 and 2008, 1,635 wire transfers totaling $517 million were sent to SIB. Pershing ceased wire transfers to SIB after numerous requests for SIB's financials went unheeded.

Stanford Capital Management's purported investment returns didn't seem to match the client statements either. Perhaps this was the most stunning revelation for a multi-billion dollar fraud. There was no real plan to cover their tracks. Investment advisors had long questioned why client returns did not closely match Stanford's reported results. For instance, individual client returns in 2000 ranged from losses of 7.7% to gains of 1.1%, yet the reported return was a gain of 18.04%. In 2001, Stanford claimed a return of 4.32%, at a time when all clients incurred losses ranging from 2.1% to 10.7%.

In fact, the investment returns were pure fabrication, reverse-engineered from investments that had never been made. Stanford and his employees simply identified outperforming funds and then calculated backwards to arrive at the rate of return that they would have earned had they actually invested in them.

They published these fictitious returns in the "pitch books" used by investment advisors to sell another Stanford product. The Stanford Allocation Strategy (SAS) was a mutual fund wrap program marketed using these bogus investment returns. These figures showed that Stanford consistently outperformed the S&P 500 by an average of 13%. The generous returns provided to advisors, along with these inflated performance statistics allowed Stanford to grow the assets under management to almost $1 billion in 2008.

Stranger still, Stanford managed to achieve identical returns of 15.71% in two years, almost statistically impossible with the supposedly diversified equity mix in its portfolio. The fantastic returns even endured the 2008 financial crisis. At a time when the S&P lost 39% and the Dow Jones STOXX Europe fell 41%, Stanford managed to limit losses to 1.3%.

When advisors questioned the returns, SGC/SCM hired an outside analyst to review the SAS fund results. The expert found that the returns were consistently overstated, a result of what he called "bad math." Despite these conclusions, SCM continued to advertise these false returns.

Now the SEC was reviewing Stanford's operations in earnest, no longer relying on the assurances provided earlier by King, Antigua's regulator back in 2003. They could no longer ignore numerous complaints from would-be investors and analysts trying to replicate Stanford's performance numbers.

Despite the pressure from the SEC, Stanford told concerned investors that the SEC's investigation was only a routine examination. He also told an investor that he could not redeem his investment because the "SEC had frozen the account for two months."

Where Were the Auditors?

Stanford could not have pulled off his fraud without the cooperation or willful blindness of the accountant who audited his firm's financial statements. The auditor was C. A. S. Hewlett, located in Hewlett House on St John's Street in St John's, Antigua.

Like many Ponzi schemes, the accounting firm employed was a tiny operation. C. A. S. Hewlett had only one practicing accountant, and an elderly one at that. Charlesworth Hewlett, nicknamed "Shelley," was born in 1936.

The septuagenarian must have been quite talented, considering that Stanford's firm paid Hewlett $4.6 million over ten years for his financial statement review and sign-off.

Despite several phone calls to Hewlett from the Securities and Exchange Commission, they were unable to reach the elusive Shelley. Was he even real? Though his existence was not refuted, he seemed remarkably difficult to reach for someone offering public accounting services.

Granted, conducting a full comprehensive audit of a multi-billion dollar company normally keeps a small army of accountants quite busy. Shelley Hewlett must have been working at breakneck speed—much too busy to return phone calls.

As more and more questions arose, news came that Mr. Hewlett had suddenly died on January 1, 2009. Details are sparse, since there was no funeral notice or other particulars. His date of death was a striking coincidence, given the December 31 year-end of the company he audited.

The Guardian, a UK newspaper, had better luck than the SEC. When the Guardian newspaper called the Hewlett office shortly after his death, the man who answered the call could not say who would take over the audit duties. Apparently, Shelley had no other qualified accountants to assume these tasks, despite the extremely lucrative fees.

Stanford's choice of auditors was perhaps the biggest red flag of all. He had used this tactic previously in Montserrat, but with less success.

Auditors apply standard tests to validate a company's financial results and ensure they are prepared in compliance with generally accepted accounting principles. As part of the annual audit, auditors independently validate account balances, test transactions, and sample controls before giving their opinion on the accuracy of the financial statements.

The company claimed to have $50 billion assets under management and thirty thousand clients in 131 countries, yet it employed a tiny local accounting firm with about a dozen employees for its annual audit. It would simply be impossible for such a small operation to perform an adequate review of Stanford's 30 offices in the US and other global locations.

Other warning signs abounded at the bank well before its demise. One job applicant reported being astounded at the limited work experience of the senior executives. Management seemed to handpick less knowledgeable people so they wouldn't have a clue about the financial shenanigans. Or perhaps they did comprehend the fraud, but knew their lack of qualifications would never land them such a senior position in a legitimate bank. Of course, many of them were complicit in the fraud and later found guilty by the courts.

The End

Years before Stanford's Ponzi scheme finally came to a head in 2009, there were many warning signs as well as a few whistleblowers. They all went unheeded. Even the SEC seemed to ignore Stanford's antics until Madoff's scheme was uncovered.

The lack of transparency and disclosure for the portfolio assets was a concern. The bulk of the portfolio consisted of non-publicly traded real estate assets, held at a time when real estate values had plummeted. But people implicitly trusted Stanford—to their ultimate detriment.

In March, 2012, Stanford was convicted of thirteen of the fourteen fraud charges against him in a Houston court. In the same month, the National Honors Committee of Antigua and Barbuda stripped Stanford of his knighthood in a unanimous vote. Three months later, he was sentenced to 110 years in prison.

Stanford now spends his days in prison at the Coleman Penitentiary near Orlando, Florida. The former Sir Allen is now simply known as inmate #35017-183. He is not likely to live to see his release date of April 17, 2105.

CHAPTER 13

PONZI #2—MMM

Ponzi Particulars	Sergey Pantelevich Mavrodi
Theme	MMM, financing office equipment
Fraud	$10 Billion US
Promised return	1,000%+
Investors defrauded	15 million
Date discovered	1994
Where	Russia
Prison sentence	4.5 years and a 10,000 ruble ($390 US) fine

Golubkov's Dream—Moscow—Spring 1994

MAVRODI STOOD IN THE DOORWAY and marveled at the stacks of cash piled from floor to ceiling. Money filled the room, and he still had a hard time believing it was real. To think it was just one room of several! Just six months ago, the bank had refused to lend him even a few thousand rubles. Now he had more money than they did. He was taking in $50 million a day, and that was only in Moscow.

Thousands of new investors arrived daily, waiting patiently to hand over their money. Everyone knew about MMM and its promise of riches. Mavrodi was the most popular man in Moscow. Especially since yesterday, after he had paid the fares of every Moscow transit user for an entire day.

Mavrodi was a mathematician by training but an entrepreneur at heart. He had finally found a lucrative business. Only a few years ago he had been barely scraping by selling pirated videos and cassettes on the streets of Moscow.

Now there were no limits to what he could achieve. He planned to expand MMM into other countries. The company had blossomed far beyond his wildest dreams, thanks to the hugely successful advertising campaign that had spread throughout the world like wildfire. The commercials featured Lyonya Golubkov, a likeable everyman who had struck it rich with Mavrodi's scheme. Though Golubkov was fictional, his success had made him the most famous man in Moscow.

You could not watch television without seeing one of the 2,500 commercials about simple Golubkov and his rags to riches story. The drab-looking tractor operator appeared to have more money than he knew what to do with. People tended to forget he was merely an actor.

Almost immediately after investing in MMM certificates, the actor told of how he was able to buy his wife new boots and a fur coat. As his investments prospered, the commercials showed him traveling to San Francisco to see Russia in the World Cup. He was pictured riding the cable cars and visiting the Golden Gate Bridge. Other commercials showed him counting endless bags of money with friends and family at a time when Russian inflation ran at 25% per month (300% per year). How did he make a 3,000% return? He did it by investing in MMM.

This portrayal of Golubkov made him something of a cult figure. MMM took Russia by storm and soon people who were eager to share in the profits lined up at MMM offices.

A Ruble Saved, a Ruble Earned

Many frauds are born out of opportunity. Mix in greed and a slim chance of prosecution and you have the perfect recipe for fraud. The MMM Ponzi scheme was the largest Ponzi scheme in history for almost twenty years until it was surpassed by Bernard Madoff's fraud in 2011.

While officially Sergey Mavrodi's fraud is the first runner-up to Bernard Madoff's Ponzi, this might be understating what the actual known numbers imply. Mavrodi had several such schemes, and if we combine them all, the total might very well surpass Madoff's fraud. MMM is still active today, in different countries and in a modified form. A simple Internet search will net you many MMM references and websites.

But are the current MMM's actually Ponzi schemes? At the very least, they are pyramid schemes, which Mavrodi has admitted to at various times. As of the writing of this book, there is an MMM scheme gathering steam in India. Mavrodi also plans to expand into China. The secret to success for Mavrodi is to take in modest amounts from as many people as possible, and to stay within the letter of the law, if not the intent.

Is a pyramid scheme the same as a Ponzi scheme? Both take money from later investors and payoff early investors. A Ponzi scheme takes it a step further. In a Ponzi scheme, the operator diverts some of that money for himself. In a Ponzi scheme, investors may or may not actively recruit new investors under them;

in a pyramid scheme, they must recruit to receive the promised payout.

While it might be unethical to take a person's money for a pyramid scheme, it is legal to do so in many parts of the world. Mavrodi is very careful to structure his investment opportunities as pyramid schemes. In doing so, he has been able to escape prosecution every time except for the first fraud, which we will look at here.

The first MMM scheme began in Russia, shortly after Gorbachev's "glasnost" policy and the "perestroika" movement took hold in the late 1980s. The terms, translated as openness and economic restructuring respectively, resulted in dramatic changes to the Soviet economy.

Russia in the 1990s was like the American Wild West, except that the frontier was a financial one. It was new territory as the state-controlled economy gave way to privatization of state-owned assets.

For some people, the new environment was like winning the lottery. Suddenly opportunities abounded that had never existed before—chances to strike it rich, or at least make some money. While the new financial frontier brought promises of riches, the sudden loosening of the grips on a central state-run economy also brought hyperinflation.

In the early 1990s, inflation ran as high as 25% per month. In 1994, prices were 2,000% higher than they had been just three years earlier. Suddenly a Moscovite with a decent retirement nest egg saw the value of his savings vaporize overnight. Now he could barely buy a loaf of bread with that same money.

Ponzi #2—MMM

It wasn't bad for everyone. Those with good connections bought government assets for practically nothing. As state assets changed into private hands, the Russian oligarchs were born. But it wasn't the only way to capitalize on the economic changes.

As state-owned assets were privatized, free enterprise grew further. This drove a need for capital markets and financing to foster business growth and investment. Unfortunately, the markets grew much faster than the regulatory oversight necessary to ensure adequate investor protection. It was also new territory for the ordinary Russian, who had never traded stocks or even used personal checks, things we take for granted in a free market economy.

Russia had no securities regulator, and the newly established Department of Securities and Financial Markets had very little real power. Protective laws, regulations, and precedents were not yet in place. It was inside this vacuum that MMM and other financial schemes blossomed. Russia went from state-controlled to unbridled capitalism almost overnight. Without the checks and balances of a financial watchdog, promoters were largely free to set their own rules. Coupled with the collective financial naiveté of a society unaccustomed to capitalism, it was fertile ground for a Ponzi scheme.

Mavrodi took advantage of the lack of regulatory supervision in the markets. MMM's promise of amazing rates was even more tantalizing when compared to the rampant inflation that was eroding Russians' savings. People flocked to the investment that promised a return that outpaced inflation.

The MMM name was derived from the initials of Sergei Mavrodi, his brother Vyachesalv Mavrodi, and Olga Melnikova. The three started the fund in 1989, but it did not become a Ponzi scheme until later in 1994.

MMM's main business was importing computer and office equipment. However, by 1994 the company found it difficult to obtain credit to finance operations. Unable to get traditional bank financing, it turned to private investors to provide the capital needed, promising them generous returns.

MMM seemed to be a runaway success. Using the investor funds as capital, the share price increased exponentially. No one questioned the fact that the share price was calculated by the very person who stood to benefit from its increase the most. There was no independent stock exchange to value the shares. Nor was the share price quoted by a third party or verified by any regulatory body. There was no trading information on the number of buyers and sellers or their asking prices. Instead, MMM calculated the stock price. Investors were happy; they did not question their thousand percent returns.

Rags to Riches

In Feb 1994, the company declared dividends of 1,000% and began an extensive advertising blitz on television featuring Lyonya Golubkov and his sudden wealth. To most Russians, the man in the commercials seemed a little simple and unsophisticated. If Golubkov could get rich, anyone could.

Mavrodi played into the thoughts and dreams

of ordinary Russians caught in the economic restructuring. Most people had seen a decrease in their standard of living while a few well-connected citizens became billionaires. The MMM commercials saturated the airwaves and featured others besides Golubkov. The younger generation identified with the newlywed couple who collected their returns, while an elderly man appealed to a more conservative, older demographic. This new social strata drove a wedge between ordinary Russians and the state. Distrust in the government grew, as did confidence in the banks and the monetary system. MMM seemed like the answer to everything.

Billions flowed into MMM over the following months, most of it in cash. In exchange for handing over their cash, participants received a paper voucher with Mavrodi's picture on it.

The company's cash receipts were more than 100 million rubles a day, too much to even count. As rubles flowed in, MMM employees resorted to estimating the amount by volume, as in "one roomful, two roomfuls", and so on.

However fantastical the returns were, they were short-lived. In July 1994, the authorities shut down MMM for tax evasion.

MMM's activities soon ground to a halt, but no one truly knew the amount owed to investors. It was speculated to be anywhere between millions and billions, but as most business was transacted in cash, it was difficult to trace and reconstruct. Many contributors faced financial ruin, and at least 50 suicides were blamed on the scheme. By Mavrodi's own accounts, he took in $10 billion from 15 million investors. Yet MMM was bankrupt.

When authorities eventually searched Mavrodi's apartment, they found little of value, and nothing to differentiate him from any other Russian, other than his butterfly collection. Where had all the money gone? Either he had spirited it out of the country, or else the authorities had missed it. Interestingly enough, he pledged to sell his $1.5 million in Gazprom stock holdings and contribute the proceeds to the unlucky MMM investors.

Once Mavrodi was charged, he decided to run for government, since as an elected official he would be immune from prosecution. Part of his platform was laying blame on the government for the lost money. He also promised $10 million in civic upgrades in greater Moscow. Voters—most of whom were also unfortunate MMM investors—bought this argument.

In 1995, Mavrodi won a seat in the Russian State Duma. His immunity was short-lived, because the government cancelled his immunity shortly thereafter. He then ran for president in a second bid to escape prosecution, but withdrew his bid for office when his nomination signatures were deemed ineligible.

Mavrodi disappeared just as MMM officially declared bankruptcy in 1997. He vanished from sight but soon started another scheme called Stock Generation, run from the tiny Caribbean country of Dominica. The online pyramid scheme operated for about two years, collecting another $5.5 million from thousands of investors in the US and elsewhere.

Stock Generation investors supposedly bought

"virtual companies." Although it promised investors a guaranteed return, Mavrodi structured it as a gambling site in order to fall outside any SEC regulations.

He ran this company while "hiding" in plain sight. He continued to live in Moscow, in an apartment by the Frunzenskaya metro station, until his eventual capture in 2003.

In April 2007, Mavrodi was finally convicted. He was sentenced to 4.5 years in prison, and fined a mere 10,000 rubles ($390 US). Given that he had been in custody since his 2003 arrest, he was released a month later due to time already served.

Since his release, he has started at least two more schemes, cheekily labeled MMM. Scheme MMM-2011 operated in Russia until May 2012, and MMM also operated in Lithuania, Ukraine, and Belarus.

The Ukranian version launched in January 2011 using the same MMM acronym and claimed millions of participants. This time, MMM stood for "We Can Do a Lot" (My Mozhem Mnogoe in Russian). In addition to a get-rich-quick scheme, it was marketed as a way to strike back against so-called government cheating and exploitation.

Mavrodi carefully structured his schemes according to the prevailing laws to avoid prosecution. He kept all monetary transactions in the accounts of the investors themselves. He substituted the vouchers used in the 1990s scheme for units of virtual money, called *mavry*, which constantly fluctuated in value. *Mavry* could be sold at any time, and the difference between the purchase price and the proceeds was how the contributor earned income.

Mavrodi's agent promised the contributor a return of the amount invested within two weeks and an additional bonus after a month, for a profit of almost 80% in just one month. The profits consisted of a series of payments specifically designed to entice people to keep their money invested. The longer the investment, the greater profits received.

This scheme had at least six levels. The ordinary investors were at the bottom. The next level, *desiatniki* (literally supervisors of ten, though they might have dozens or more under them), recruited investors and received a 10% cut of each new contribution. Each *desiatniki* was responsible only for their recruits, and they also executed all financial transactions for them, including payouts. In turn, the *desiatniki* reported to the *sotniki* level above, who had authority over several *desiatniki* groups. This continued up several more levels, with each taking a cut. Mavrodi sat at the top of the structure.

The structure meant that most transactions did not flow through or to Mavrodi. Payments funneled through the many people below him instead. If Mavrodi was charged and prosecuted, it would be impossible to undo all the transactions and prove his wrongdoing.

Mavrodi soon ran into cash flow issues, since there was no underlying investment. He then announced Operation Phoenix, slashing returns to 10% per month and cancelling signing bonuses. As contributors panicked and MMM collapsed, Mavrodi started up yet another MMM scheme, supposedly to help those stuck in the current scheme.

Ponzi #2—MMM

Mavrodi has expanded even further. At the time of writing in 2013, MMM India, known there as Mavrodi Mondial Moneybox India, was actively courting investors. Several MMM promoters were arrested in June 2013, and Mavrodi confirmed that they were his associates. He also stated his intent to expand into China. He quite obviously wants to target populous countries.

Mavrodi claims he is not out to personally enrich himself. He states:

> "My goal is a financial apocalypse, a destruction of the global financial system. I consider the current financial system unfair; it's not fair that some people own billions while others have nothing. The system must be destroyed and something else must be built in its place. That's precisely what I'm working on."

One thing is certain—his schemes result in financial disaster for most participants, though he always seems to emerge unscathed. While Mavrodi purports to operate a revolutionary network that lifts people out of poverty, nothing could be further from the truth. Every MMM scheme eventually goes bankrupt, taking the savings of many gullible people along with it.

The promises of guaranteed returns might be false, but one thing is certain. Mavrodi, and people like him, will still be operating, skirting the law, and finding new ways to part people from their money.

CHAPTER 14

PONZI #1

BERNARD MADOFF—HEDGE YOUR BETS

Ponzi Particulars	Bernard Madoff
Theme	Bernard L. Madoff Investment Securities LLC, stock options strategy
Fraud	$65 Billion US
Promised return	10%+ per year
Investors defrauded	2,500+
Date discovered	2008
Where	New York, New York
Prison sentence	150 years

New York—December 10, 2008

BERNARD MADOFF STOOD AT THE curved glass windows of his midtown Manhattan office in the Lipstick building and stared out towards the East River and Trump World Tower. Movement on the street below caught his eye. Commuters and early Christmas shoppers scurried along the sidewalks like ants, oblivious to his dilemma. Some of them might have even had money in his fund, indirectly through one of the feeder funds.

No matter what he did, people would soon know he no longer had the money to pay them back. Whatever small amount remained he needed to hold onto for himself. He had created immense wealth for everyone else, basically from nothing. Millions, even billions, would soon slip through his fingers for the very last time.

At 70 years old, the former non-executive chairman of the NASDAQ stock market knew he was too old to start over again. He wished the financial crisis had happened later, after he had retired. Of course, deep in his heart he knew nobody ever retired from a game like this.

He had been staving off angry investors for weeks. Instead of new investors begging to invest in his funds, his biggest longtime investors were requesting redemptions—some for hundreds of millions. The asset-backed commercial paper crisis, followed by the real estate meltdown, had resulted in a cash crunch.

Since the financial tides had turned, all the big fish wanted to liquidate. They were caught in the financial crisis liquidity squeeze just as he was. The banks were in trouble too. He didn't have enough cash to ride out the storm.

The financial crisis and subsequent Lehman Brothers collapse had severely impacted his ability to bring in new capital. Over one hundred hedge funds that held capital with Lehman were effectively frozen, increasing a ripple effect worldwide. It was the same in Europe too. No one had liquidity. Those who did have cash were not willing to risk parting with it for any reason. Not to lend, and certainly not to invest.

There were even questions about how he could have possibly earned such outsized returns in a declining market. Everyone else was losing, so why hadn't he experienced losses?

Ponzi #1Bernard Madoff—Hedge Your Bets

Madoff had claimed it was his derivative option strategy, but as the whole market tanked, that claim became harder and harder to defend. Some analysts had reverse-engineered his investment strategy, only to come up with large losses instead of gains. He remained silent and unavailable, but the mainstream financial media was starting to pick up on the rumblings and suspicions.

Many of his current investors were still blissfully unaware that he no longer had their money, but he had run out of excuses for not honoring their redemption requests on a timely basis. He knew what had to be done. His decision meant that it would all come crashing down tomorrow, so he intended to enjoy the last few hours while he could.

The public would no longer think of him as a great Wall Street statesman. He would be exposed as a financial pariah instead. His legacy bothered him more than anything. His track record was legendary and no one had been able to match his performance. More than a few hedge funds had invested everything with him rather than do any research or find other investments themselves. They knew they could never replicate his stellar returns. He had worked this juggling act for decades, except now he had too many balls in the air. His only regret was not planning a better exit strategy. Nevertheless, in some strange way he was actually relieved at what he was about to do.

Coming clean would take the pressure off. He would lose some of his immense wealth and no doubt a few friends. Then he would beg forgiveness, wait for the furor to die down and lie low at the Madoff mansion in Florida or maybe their pied-à-terre on the French Riviera. A good lawyer, a hefty fine and a plea deal and he would soon have this mess behind him.

Madoff turned from his aerie and scanned his spotless office, his refuge for over twenty years. The clean black-and-white tones calmed the churning in his stomach. One phone call and all hell would break loose. His life would change forever.

But not quite yet.

Bernard Madoff sighed and flipped through the freshly signed checks. One hundred checks totaling $173 million, all that remained of the billions invested in his fund. Not nearly enough to go around, and whatever was left had to be spent wisely to curry favor with the right people. He would placate those who might cover for him, or at least keep mum. He had to contain this thing as much as possible. The checks took care of the most powerful in his circle. In the coming days, he would need all the help he could get from them.

Overnight his friends would become enemies. While he couldn't make the feeder funds whole, he could at least ensure his friends and family retained something. He picked up his Mont Blanc pen and jotted a note to send his watches and Ruth's jewelry to the kids, out of the clutches of the authorities.

Unlike the SEC investigation more than a decade ago, the regulators had not knocked at his door this time. In fact, they were blissfully ignorant of his decades-old fraud, though he had been operating under their eyes for years.

He chuckled as he recalled inept investigators combing his offices while he stole billions in plain sight, right out from under their noses. Their examiners pored over fake trade tickets, fabricated investment statements and a tangled web of wire transfers back and forth amongst his various bank accounts. Not one detected a trace of his deceit.

This time was different. With his capital dried up, he could no longer meet the now massive redemption requests on his fund. The lie was so huge that there was simply no other way out. Turning himself in was his only option.

Albeit slim, he figured there was a chance he could emerge from this almost unscathed. A good lawyer and voluntary disclosure would definitely make a difference.

He had found himself in similar circumstances before. When the SEC stumbled onto him in 1996, it had been through Avelino & Bienes, the CPA firm that had fed money into his fund. His recordkeeping had met the test, because he had been careful to keep all the incriminating evidence at a distance. The bumbling agents sniffed around and never got too close, but it could have been much worse. His lawyer contained the mess, and all Avelino & Bienes had to do was give the investors back their principal investment amount.

Those SEC investigators would have trouble spotting a scam if they tripped over it. One of them almost had. The second, most recent investigation had resulted in a marriage between his niece, who also worked at the firm, and one of the SEC investigators.

Luckily, the New York financial sector was incestuous to a fault, and these inter-relationships cemented his position as unassailable. Most SEC staff would give their shirts to work in a firm like his. Their salary would double overnight, and in a couple of years, they would be millionaires.

He felt a little like God, knowing that his confession tomorrow would unleash panic on Wall Street. There would be a ripple effect, even with those who hadn't invested in his fund. His actions alone would lead to the undoing of many millionaires, billionaires, and even other hedge funds. Of course, it was completely their fault for both trusting him and concentrating all their wealth with him in the first place.

He glanced at his black-faced Philippe Patek watch. The silver hands pointed to Roman numerals spelling out five o'clock. He absently rubbed the alligator strap, wondering if Ruth was back from shopping yet.

He glanced toward the door and spotted a crooked picture frame. He frowned. A world without order and structure was chaos. His office reflected that sense of order, decorated in monochrome, clean lines. Both his New York and London offices were in black, white, or shades of gray. His private jet was the same.

He rose from the black conference table and strode over to level the frame. The prints were all of bulls. They were a reminder to him—and to others—of his success on Wall Street. Like the rest of the décor, the prints were all in black and white.

He froze when he discovered the smeared fingerprint on the surface. It concerned him on several levels. He did not like sloppiness, and everyone knew better than to touch his things. He would complain to his assistant about the mess tomorrow.

But it was more than the crooked picture frame. His sense of unease grew and his pulse quickened when he realized that the few employees allowed on his floor knew better than to touch his things. Someone else had obviously been in here. Who?

On second thought, by this time tomorrow it would no longer matter.

This floor was the domain of his private hedge fund, off limits to almost everybody in the firm. Most employees occupied the lower two floors, where the legitimate trading arm of Bernard L. Madoff securities operated.

He glanced at his watch again, wondering where Ruth wanted to go for dinner tonight. He walked slowly back to the conference table and lit another Davidoff cigar. It was the only thing calming his nerves today. He took his seat at the head of the table and studied the checks before him. The recipients couldn't stay angry forever once they realized the favor he had done them. They might hate him for a while, until they realized they had recovered more than most.

Most of the checks were destined for well-connected business associates who had provided billions of capital over the years. Whether their own money, or funneled through their own feeder hedge funds was irrelevant. The checks bought loyalty, and he chose the recipients carefully. The payees were a who's-who of the rich and powerful, heads of foundations and charitable organizations, prominent socialites and tycoons. In short, people who made better allies than enemies. Once things settled down, they would be back at the trough, begging to invest with him again.

The rest of the investors would not likely even see a dime. He certainly wasn't about to let government bureaucrats decide how to divvy up what little money was left. Everyone lost in the financial crisis, but the checks showed that for those who really mattered, he had placed their needs first, right up there with his family.

He took a long pull from his cigar and slowly exhaled. Was there another option he hadn't considered? Maybe a golf trip to line up more investor money? He didn't want to pull the plug if he didn't have to.

No—everybody was tapped out. If there were any money to be had, he would have found it by now. The jig was up. In the end it was probably better this way. He had been trying to figure out an alternative for weeks now, but there were no other options. Once he turned himself in, he would be on the hook for at least a hefty fine. But with a plea deal he'd recover.

Rotten to the Core

Midtown Manhattan's Lipstick building at 885 Third Avenue was, and still is, a New York Landmark. The rose glass and reddish brown granite façade was pretty on the outside, but it disguised a rotten core. Corruption permeated the offices of Bernard L. Madoff Securities LLC, stretching from the seventeenth to the nineteenth floors.

Was the fictionalized account really how Madoff made his fateful decision to turn himself in? We will probably never know for sure. What we do know is that the cash to keep the scheme going had dried up with the financial crisis.

It is hard to believe how so many family members and employees working at Madoff's firm could have been completely in the dark. By all appearances, they were a very close bunch. Many had worked there for decades and there were at least a few office romances. It defies logic that all the financial shenanigans remained compartmentalized.

While Madoff's surroundings were black and white, nothing about him was that clear-cut. He was a stickler for details, at least about his office décor and expensive jewelry. Perhaps telling, he never seemed to spend any time on the computer, poring over financial reports, or doing anything else resembling trading activity. No need to, since he had not done any trading whatsoever in at least thirteen years.

It would be extremely difficult to manage a legitimate multi-billion dollar fund with the less than thirty employees Madoff employed. Even more unbelievable is Madoff's claim that he carried out the fraud alone and unaided. Assuming he covered his tracks and somehow duped his employees, despite never using anything other than a phone, how did he single-handedly manage to create fake trade tickets, fabricate investor statements, and wire money through circuitous routes without arousing suspicion?

Was he telling the entire truth at the end, or covering up for others? Anyone who cheats clients and close friends alike over a span of decades is likely selective about the truth.

How did he carry out daily fraud activities despite

his frequent trips away on his private jet or yacht?
Madoff did not provide details, probably for good
reason. Lack of evidence makes it harder to piece
together the case against him. The less he said, the
harder it would be to trace all the assets. The end
result? Not just a weaker case, but the possibility of
still undiscovered assets.

The Madoffs appear to have lost most of their
assets, but it is hard to believe Madoff didn't have a
backup plan. Astonishingly, he seems to have had no
retirement savings.

Some suspect offshore money stashed in nominee
accounts, but retrieving it now would only attract the
attention of the Madoff trustee assigned to recover
what crumbs remain from the massive fraud.

We already know Madoff attempted to hide assets.
Just before his Ponzi scheme imploded, he wrote
checks to favored people. Madoff and his wife also
mailed over a million dollars worth of jewelry to their
sons and others after his house arrest.

He also had a habit of transferring assets into wife
Ruth's name, as he did in the 1996 SEC investigation.

No "I" in Team

Madoff claimed to have carried out his Ponzi
scheme completely unaided. He might have wanted
to shield his family (and more importantly, the family
assets), but his attempt to protect others probably
came with an ulterior motive. Maybe he hoped certain
individuals would funnel funds back to his family
after hearing of the seized assets.

As an ex-employee of the SEC and a Wall Street

veteran, Madoff knew the ropes. He needed underlying transaction records to back up his claimed investment returns, so he set about manufacturing them. Just like Allen Stanford, he determined what the return would be, then reverse-engineered everything, starting with the trade tickets to substantiate the transactions, and culminating with the financial statements that ultimately reported the firm's profits.

Consider the sheer volume of record-keeping necessary to keep everything straight and appear legitimate. Madoff had to produce fictitious financial statements, with supporting documentation adequate to pass the scrutiny of the several SEC audits he underwent over the decades.

When investors wired money in or requested redemptions, someone had to process the transaction. Despite Madoff's initial claims, we now have confirmation that he received help from others, notably people in his accounting department. In fact, it was truly a team effort, with secrets passed on to replacement staff as people retired.

Irwin Lipkin, Madoff's very first employee, was hired in 1964 as financial controller. He retired in 1998, but prior to that had falsified records. He also testified that Madoff continued to pay him for several years after he retired. Was it to buy his silence?

Enrica Cotellessa-Pitz, who replaced Lipkin upon his retirement, admitted to falsifying accounting records and financial statements. Coincidentally, she also oversaw the company's anti-money laundering program. Cotellessa-Pitz started working for Madoff's firm thirty years ago, and admitted to altering records after she assumed the controller position.

David Kugel, a supervisor in the firm's proprietary trading area, helped create fictitious backdated trades by supplying historical prices to two other employees. These were then used as backup to the fabricated trades.

Craig Kugel, David's son, also worked at Madoff's firm in human resources. While he wasn't directly involved in the Ponzi scheme, he participated in other fraudulent activities, including paying people not actively working at the company and falsifying U.S. Labor department filings. He also charged personal expenses on his company credit card.

Eric Lipkin, son of Irwin Lipkin, joined his father at Madoff's firm and also falsified records. They also profited from working for Madoff, earning generous salaries, and holding investment accounts at the firm where they withdrew more money than they put in.

As of August 2013, David Kugel and both Lipkins have been permanently barred from working in the securities sector by the SEC. They are awaiting sentencing.

Madoff was also generous to a fault—with other people's money.

Interspersed with all these crimes were numerous credit card transactions for expensive baubles, trips, vacations, and other luxuries. Madoff even bought a home for a longtime employee using $2.7 million of company funds. Few bosses go to that extent for their employees. In the unlikely event they did, how many would pay for it out of their personal bank account?

Madoff also employed a number of family members. Peter Madoff, his brother, was the firm's Chief Compliance Officer. Peter's daughter also served as Compliance Officer. Madoff's two sons, Mark and Andrew, also worked at the firm, though both denied any knowledge of the fraud. Eldest son Mark committed suicide after the Ponzi scheme was exposed.

Marion Madoff, Peter Madoff's wife, had a "no show" job at the company. Despite not working at Madoff Securities LLC, she was paid an annual salary of $163,500. While many company owners do pay spouses a salary in perhaps questionable circumstances, Peter was not a part owner of his brother's business. He was merely one of his brother's highly paid and under qualified employees, albeit one that actually showed up at the office.

The Scam

Bernard Madoff was arrested and convicted of running the biggest Ponzi scheme in recorded history. His scheme is the biggest fraud of the 21st century—at least so far.

Madoff's superior returns were the stuff of legend, and almost everyone wanted into his exclusive funds. His fund had consistently averaged a 12% return annually for decades. This result was remarkable, given several very sharp market corrections over the years his firm had been in operation. How did he perform so well in good times and bad? Or rather, how did he claim to have done so?

Madoff claimed to use a strategy called a split-strike conversion, also known as a collar. This strategy employs stock options to limit both the losses and the gains for an investment in a particular stock. A stock option is a bet on an underlying stock, giving you the right to buy or sell a stock at a particular price that may be higher or lower than the stock's current trading price. A call option gives you the right to buy a stock. If the stock is trading higher than the call option's exercise price, the call option becomes more valuable. Conversely if the stock is trading below the call option exercise price (called a strike price), the stock option drops in value and might become worthless, since these options have a limited life.

While purchasing the stock options adds additional expense, it also limits the risk (and reward) by locking in the upper and lower price limits at which you can buy or sell the stock.

Madoff's split-strike strategy supposedly invested in S&P stocks that closely followed the overall S&P index. Most of these stocks also paid dividends. In addition to call options, he also employed put options, which give you the right to sell the underlying stock at a predetermined price.

Here is an example. Say you buy a stock at $20 that pays 60 cents in annual dividends. You also want to lock in your downside risk, so you buy a put option. This allows you to sell that same stock at a pre-determined price. You buy this option to sell the stock at close to the current stock price, say at $18. You pay $1 for this option, which guarantees you can sell the stock at the $18 price, even if the stock drops to zero. You have now locked in at least an $18 selling price, a maximum $2 loss from your $20 purchase price. You can exercise that option if the stock drops below $18. However, your upside remains potentially limitless, because the value of your holding increases as long as you continue to hold the stock. In effect, you are buying insurance against loss.

You have already decided that you will sell the stock at $25, since you have determined that this price is likely to be the stock's upside price potential. Since you have already decided on an exit point, why not profit now by locking in a $25 selling price with a buyer ahead of time? This is essentially what you are doing by selling a covered call option. Covered means you are selling an option to buy stock you already own.

This covered call option is the second part of the split-strike conversion. You sell a call for $25, giving the buyer the right to buy the stock from you in the future at $25. Your $25 price is well above the current stock price to limit the probability of it being exercised in the near future. For this strategy, you collect a $2 call option premium from the buyer. Meanwhile you continue to hold the stock until the stock price exceeds the $25 strike price, at which point the buyer exercises his option and you surrender your stock to him for a $25 payment. Often this exercise never happens, and the seller of the option (you) simply keeps the option premium income. This strategy can make small but consistent profits over time.

We will use a simplistic example of the above with an investment that was held for exactly one year, with options contracts employed on the purchase date, and dividends paid annually exactly one year after purchase. We further assume that our option assumptions were correct and so held the stock without exercising the options:

Split-strike Conversion Example—Stock Price Increases

Date	Security	Cash Inflow (Outflow)	Net
January 1	Purchase Price	($20.00)	
January 1	Put Option Purchased	($1.00)	
Investment			($21.00)
January 1	Call Option Sold	$2.00	
December 31	Dividend	$0.60	
December 31	Sale Price	$25.00	
Proceeds			$27.60
Gain (Loss) on Investment			$6.60
Gain (Loss) %			31.4%

Madoff's premise was that the options provided the basis for his remarkably consistent returns by decreasing the volatility and risk.

In theory at least, it is quite an effective strategy. In reality, it depends on how much you pay for the options, and the eventual outcome of the underlying stock price. There must be both a buyer and a seller at the desired prices. In practice, it might be very difficult to get a large enough spread to offset the cost of the options. Additionally, if you are unable to find a counterparty, you cannot complete the transaction to exercise your strategy.

If Madoff was able to obtain outsized returns employing the above strategy on the NYSE, why didn't other funds follow suit to achieve similar returns? Profitable strategies rarely remain secret for long.

Madoff also reported consistent gains month after month, year after year, despite fluctuating markets. Even if this strategy was as successful as he claimed, it would not always enable the investor to lock in gains and eliminate losses. Let's look at the above example again, only this time we will assume the stock price actually dropped to $16. We then would have exercised the put option for the following result:

Split-strike Conversion
Example—Stock Price Decreases

Date	Security	Cash Inflow (Outflow)	Net
January 1	Purchase Price	($20.00)	
January 1	Put Option Purchased	($1.00)	
Investment			($21.00)
January 1	Call Option Sold	$2.00	
December 31	Dividend	$0.60	
December 31	Sale Price (Exercise of Put)	$18.00	
Proceeds			$20.60

Gain (Loss) on Investment			($0.40)
Gain (Loss) %			(1.9%)

The split-strike strategy does not guarantee gains. It minimizes volatility or the extent of the losses, but not the direction. A loss will still be a loss, albeit a smaller loss, since your put allows you to sell the stock at a locked-in price. Buying options lowers the overall volatility, but the expense of the options also means a lower overall return.

Using the split-strike example above, the return could have ranged from a 31.4% gain to an 1.9% loss. Investing in the stock directly without the options strategy would have netted a 25% return or a 23.8% loss.

In summary, the strategy will reduce upside return (due to the cost of the protective put option), but also minimize loss. What it does not do is eliminate a loss from happening in the first place.

There were several severe market corrections during Madoff's investment time horizon where all stocks suffered a loss. It would have been impossible for Madoff's funds not to realize losses during these periods of market decline.

Even professional money managers were in the dark about Madoff's fraud, as much of the money invested came from other "feeder" hedge funds. As a result, many individuals discovered that their supposedly safe investment was in fact in a feeder fund to Madoff's.

Ponzi #1Bernard Madoff—Hedge Your Bets

What is remarkable is that these feeder funds did not detect the multi-decade fraud, or ask basic questions. They were unconcerned as long as the money kept rolling in. Instead of time-consuming investment research, they could simply park their clients' money in Bernie's fund and head for the golf course. The returns continued as they always had—a win-win for the fund manager and their clients. How could you go wrong with guaranteed returns?

We know how that eventually turned out. But why hadn't anyone exposed Madoff sooner? As a well-connected former NASDAQ chairman, was his reputation above reproach? Perhaps he was simply too powerful, able to make or break careers with a few well-placed words in the right places. Some competitors and potential investors reported their suspicions to the SEC. The SEC performed several investigations, but with inconclusive results.

Despite the many red flags and several persistent whistleblowers, the SEC turned a blind eye most of the time. When they did investigate, they did so only at a cursory level. While the reasons behind their actions go beyond the scope of this book, one simple reason Madoff escaped closer scrutiny was that people rarely question good fortune until it goes bad. Many of Madoff's cynics simply walked away, choosing not to invest. They assumed the regulator had or would exercise appropriate oversight and action.

Askia LLC, a hedge fund consultant, had previously reviewed and advised against investing in the funds that fed into Madoff's fund. Jim Vos, CEO and Head of Research, and Jake Waltour, Head of Advisory

Services, issued a statement to investors shortly after the Madoff fraud was exposed.

While they did not study Madoff's own fund, they did examine the feeder funds that fed into Madoff's. As a result of this due diligence, they decided not to invest in the feeder funds.

Their statement cited many factors that formed the basis of their earlier recommendation not to invest. These factors seem glaringly obvious once identified. Some of their red flags included:

1. Askia's in-house analyst reverse-engineered the feeder funds' purported transactions, but found they could not replicate the returns using Madoff's methodology. For one thing, the S&P options market was simply too small to accommodate the sheer volume of trades needed to produce the returns claimed for his multi-billion dollar fund.

2. Despite the feeder funds' large size and use of well-known auditors and administrators, the fund custodian was Madoff Securities itself. This is highly unusual, as third-party custodians are usually used. They segregate the physical custody of the investments from the investment manager. This caused Askia to undertake further due diligence. A review of the audit uncovered another alarming fact. Madoff used a three-person accounting firm to audit his multi-billion fund, of which only one employee was a practicing accountant.

It would be impossible for one accountant to audit a multi-billion dollar fund.

3. The audited financial statements of the feeder funds indicated at least $13 billion in securities, yet the required 13F securities filings showed only small amounts of stocks. Feeder fund managers claimed this was a result of a strategy to have 100% cash at quarter ends. Unwinding all of the supposedly covered positions to reach this 100% cash position defies logic. If you believe your underlying investment strategy is sound, why would you liquidate it? Even assuming there was a good reason, why cash out only at (and exactly on) quarter ends?

4. Madoff's fund transactions were paper-based, despite claims they used advanced trading technology. Feeder fund managers received the paper trade tickets by snail mail and had no electronic access to their accounts. Paper trade tickets allowed Madoff to potentially manipulate results to make them whatever he wanted them to be.

5. Madoff employed family members (two sons, a brother, and a niece) for key positions such as regulatory compliance. Feeder fund transactions were highly secretive and the details only known to a select few within the firm.

6. Madoff Securities controlled all aspects of trading, custody, and administration, either directly or through discretionary brokerage accounts. There was no segregation or independent oversight.

There was another important reason Madoff's fraud was undetected for so long. Many of his clients were endowment funds or private foundations. Private foundations are required to pay out 5% of their capital each year, and they typically do not pay out more than the minimum, in order to keep enough capital to fund in perpetuity. There was no risk of the foundation redeeming the funds as long as the fictitious returns reported were stellar. With only a 5% payout, Madoff had decades' worth of money to play with.

If the charitable foundations and other Madoff investors had performed a few simple background or reference checks, they would have also uncovered these issues. They did little or no due diligence. Instead, they were blinded by their above-average returns and Madoff's reputation as a financial genius.

Bernard Madoff was not your typical Ponzi schemer. At seventy years old, he was well known on Wall Street, having served as chair of the NASDAQ stock exchange in 1990, 1991 and 1993. Was he already successful by the time he perpetrated his fraud? Or did it begin much earlier? Could his Ponzi scheme have been the underlying reason for his success in the first place?

Wolves in the Henhouse

While the SEC's mandate is to provide independent oversight of financial markets, in reality it is very difficult for the SEC to remain completely at arm's length. Many SEC employees move on to work for Wall Street firms, enticed by salaries as much as ten times what they can make at the government agency. Most are reluctant to diligently investigate potential future employers who might someday pay them multi-million-dollar salaries. Even if they do go after the VIPs, such questioning will likely be shut down by their superiors. At the very least, such investigations can prove to be career-limiting. The mixing of jobs and opportunity has created an incestuous circle.

Madoff's niece (a compliance officer and attorney at Madoff's firm) married Eric Swanson, a former assistant director at the SEC. They met while Swanson was investigating Madoff Investment Securities LLC, one of several such investigations in the years before Madoff's 2008 arrest. While no wrongdoing was officially attributed to these two, it illustrates the all-too-cozy environment between Wall Street and the SEC.

Swanson's relationship with Shana Madoff certainly appeared to be a conflict of interest. He did not disclose their relationship to his SEC manager until April 2006 when concerns arose about the Madoff operation. Prior to that, in March 2004, an SEC lawyer who worked two levels below Swanson reported unusual trading relating to Madoff's funds. The lawyer was told to ignore the trades.

Shana Madoff has never been charged in connection

with the Ponzi scheme. However, she held a senior compliance position immediately after graduation from law school. Few new graduates can hope for such a senior position at a multi-billion dollar investment firm. Only a handful will achieve such a level after decades. Of course, having Peter Madoff, her father, as Chief Compliance Officer, helped.

Shana's responsibility as Compliance Officer was to certify the accuracy of the firm's financial records. She signed off on records showing 23 clients holding $17.1 billion dollars in assets under management. In reality, there were 1,900 investors who supposedly held investments with a current value of $68 billion.

Even a cursory look through the company ledgers would reveal a difference between 23 clients and 1,900 investors, something Ms. Madoff should have done as a basic part of her job. Either she was negligent and did not adequately perform the duties of a compliance officer, or she knew about the discrepancies. As a lawyer, she should have known that signing off on false statements was a criminal offense.

Madoff was very careful to avoid scrutiny. He refused to answer any questions, especially from other hedge fund managers dissecting or reverse engineering his scheme. His elusive nature added to the mystique; the excuse that disclosing his strategy risked copycats was effective. In reality, any details provided would allow others to reverse-engineer his trades, which of course were non-existent. Providing answers to probing questions from financial analysts would have quickly exposed him as a fraud.

While Madoff was extremely well connected,

he was careful to distance himself from the actual fundraising. He was unapproachable, and refused to discuss his investment strategies with anyone. This not only kept his hands clean, but also lent an air of exclusivity.

Whether it was due to Madoff's power as a former NASDAQ chairman or some other reason we don't know, people at the SEC seemed to look the other way.

Despite his claims, Madoff never did operate alone. While certain individuals knew more pieces of the puzzle than others, there were at least a half dozen people complicit in the fraud. Some fabricated trade tickets, some solicited new money, knowing there was no substance, and others provided audit opinions without examining the books. It was a well-oiled fraud machine. These people benefitted financially in one way or another. Madoff simply could not have pulled off a fraud of this magnitude without their help.

While Bernie Madoff claimed sole responsibility, he is no martyr. Taking the blame kept other details secret, making the criminal case harder to prove. On some level, he probably wanted to take all the credit for this decades-long fraud. The thought of outsmarting so many people gave him bragging rights.

Given Madoff was already fabulously wealthy, why did he operate a Ponzi scheme in the first place? By all appearances, he didn't need the money. He was already a billionaire. Risking arrest when he was already wealthy seemed crazy. But as we have already seen, money is rarely the sole driver to commit fraud. Ego and power often play pivotal roles, and these factors seemed to be contributors for Madoff's fraud.

There is yet another possibility. What if Madoff's pre-existing wealth wasn't what it appeared to be? What if most of his billions came not from his legitimate brokerage activities, but from earlier frauds? Could his deception have started much earlier than anyone suspected? That could certainly be the case, given some of the questionable activities underway since the 1980s.

The Accountants

To truly understand how Madoff's scheme became so large, we need to go back to those earlier times. Specifically, we should look at the accountants who enabled his early success. For a time, they were at the center of it all.

Bernard Madoff founded his investment business in 1960, shortly after his marriage to Ruth Alpern in November 1959. They were high school sweethearts, having both attended Far Rockaway High School together. According to a 50th anniversary update Ruth provided for alumni, Ruth and Bernie "worked together in the investment business he founded in 1960." She was also a director of the company.

There was yet another family connection—Madoff's firm used the services of the accounting firm founded by Ruth's father. Saul Alpern was a partner in the accounting firm Alpern & Heller. In 1962, the name changed to Alpern & Avellino upon Heller's departure and the addition of Frank Avellino to the firm. When Ruth's father eventually retired and Michael Bienes joined, the name changed to Avellino & Bienes.

The SEC investigated Avellino & Bienes in 1992. At

that time, the SEC discovered that they were acting as unregistered investment advisors by soliciting investment funds. They promised 10% returns, carefully wording the description to suggest a promissory note rather than a securities investment. As long as they were not selling securities, they figured they could operate outside of the SEC regulatory framework. The SEC thought otherwise and determined they were in fact selling securities after they examined the accounting firm's records in the early 1990s. The following excerpts are from an actual Avellino & Bienes letter to a prospective investor in August 1991:

> *Avellino & Bienes invests with one particular Wall Street Broker (the same company since we first started doing business over 25 years ago) who buys and sells stocks and bonds in the name of Avellino & Bienes. The list of securities being traded are top corporations such as IBM, AT&T, etc. It's the mechanics being used to protect the portfolio that makes our business successful, not just the top name securities being traded.*

Everything in the first paragraph implies securities investing—stocks, bonds, and securities. After name-dropping some blue-chip stocks, it mentions some vague "mechanics" that "protect" the portfolio, without mentioning exactly what those mechanics are or how they might work to generate successful investment income.

Investing with one particular (unnamed) Wall

Street Broker important enough to have their name capitalized would surely impress you, even if you were not allowed to know his name.

The only explicit statement provided is that the "investor" is Avellino & Bienes. In other words, certainly not the addressee (that is, the person handing over the money to Avellino & Bienes). The wording carefully skirts around securities regulations and registration requirements:

> *We do not encourage new accounts and therefore we do not solicit same. We do, however, like to accommodate those individuals, etc. that are recommended as you have been through Virginia Atherton. Summarily, this is a very private group and no financial statements, prospectuses or brochures have been printed or are available.*

Aren't we lucky that while they discourage our money, they are willing to do us a favor? Not everyone gets a recommendation to a club that is secret enough to take your money and never provide you with any written proof of its actual whereabouts now or in the future. They don't even encourage new accounts. But since you asked, they will "accommodate" you by taking your money.

They do not solicit investments either. An important disclaimer, since that would require them to register as an investment advisor:

> *Let me clarify one important thing. The money that is sent to A&B is a loan to A&B who in turns*

*invests it on behalf of A&B for which our clients
receive quarterly interest payments.*

This statement is a bit of legalese to categorize
your contribution as a loan rather than an investment
in stocks. Now that you have been impressed with
the opportunity to earn a return off the wonderful
and mysterious portfolio in the first paragraph,
this statement explicitly calls it a loan and not an
investment. That way it does not fall under the
scrutiny of securities laws and the SEC. If they are
not selling investments, they do not have to register
with the SEC as investment advisors or comply with
their fussy rules, such as issuing a prospectus.
Of course, whether the offering is a loan or an
investment is ultimately determined by the SEC and
securities regulations.

How many accounting firms borrow money at
exorbitant rates to buy heavily leveraged investments?
Not many. Why can't the firm simply use a bank
for loans? Surely banks would offer competitive
rates on a low-risk investment? Last but not least,
this successful firm would likely have very good
banking connections.

The red flags practically jumped off the page in
hindsight. Of course, the SEC thought so at the
time as well, and determined that Avellino & Bienes
were promoting investments in violation of the
Securities Act.

The SEC's investigation unearthed the connection
with Madoff. Avellino & Bienes promised returns of
13%-20% while turning over all the money to Mr.

Madoff. Avellino claimed they were on the hook for the stated return, no matter what actual investment return Madoff made. This claim was somewhat surprising, considering that the small accounting firm had fed $441 million to Madoff, representing 3,200 clients. An awful lot could have gone wrong, given fluctuating markets. Apparently though, it never did. Despite stock market fluctuations, there were no losses of any kind reported. None.

There were also no records to back up the claims. It is extremely unlikely that an accounting firm in particular would not keep ledgers of its' own transactions, especially multi-million dollar ones. The SEC suspected a Ponzi scheme.

Avellino & Bienes were represented by attorney Ira Sorkin. In a striking coincidence, Sorkin later became Madoff's lead defense attorney. Early in his career, Sorkin had been a staff lawyer for the SEC, and after that, a regional administrator. He had also served as a federal prosecutor. His knowledge and connections resulted in a very favorable settlement for Avellino & Bienes.

The SEC settled with the accounting firm, allowing them to simply refund all the investors their money. Avellino and Bienes each got a slap on the wrist: after admitting they were unregistered investment advisors, they closed down, paid the audit firm's costs, and a $350,000 fine.

Madoff, at the time, claimed that Avellino & Bienes was a feeder fund and that he had no idea they were unregistered. Funneling the money through Avellino & Bienes proved to be the perfect cover for

Madoff, since it insulated him from the prying eyes of regulators. Since they got a cut off the top, Avellino & Bienes were enriched in the process. At the time this all transpired, Madoff was chairman of the NASDAQ stock exchange.

In retrospect, the Avellino & Bienes investors were very lucky. According to the FBI press release of March 10, 2009, Madoff's Ponzi scheme had been in operation since at least the 1980s. These Avellino & Bienes investors would likely have still had their money invested in Madoff's fund if the SEC had not shut the Avellino & Bienes feeder fund down. In theory at least, the later Madoff investors could be owed a portion of the money that was returned to the Avellino & Bienes investors, since all monies recovered should be divided pro rata. The Avellino & Bienes investors received a 100% refund, while Madoff's other investors received little or nothing at all.

Madoff's luck seemed endless. The Avellino & Bienes fraud investigation did not progress further. He carried on, business as usual, except he had to find another accounting firm since Avellino & Bienes had shut down. He turned to another friend, Jerome Horowitz, who operated a tiny accounting firm with his son-in-law, David Friehling. After Horowitz retired, Friehling became the sole auditor for Madoff's multi-billion dollar business.

This was an interesting move, given that Friehling did not have clearance to perform audits from the American Society of Certified Public Accountants, the governing body for accountants in the United States.

Auditors not only require approval from this governing body, they must also participate in a peer review process to have their work validated by other audit firms. It is a compliance and oversight check, providing assurance of competency and independence.

Friehling had provided written confirmation to the American Society of Public Accountants that his firm did not perform audits. Yet he provided an audit opinion on the Madoff statements. He later admitted he had not performed an audit—he had simply rubber-stamped the financial statements as audited.

In addition to lying about the audits, Friehling had a conflict of interest, since he had personally invested with Madoff. Auditors are prohibited from auditing companies in which they have self-interest.

For his transgressions, Friehling was rewarded with a lengthy prison sentence. He also forfeited his CPA certification, and was barred from practicing as an accountant again. While Friehling was punished for lying about the nonexistent audit, no one seemed to notice that Madoff's firm had escaped an audit, which would have entailed the examination of his firm's books and records. Without an audit, once more Madoff was off the hook. His biggest problem was searching for another cooperative accounting firm.

Why didn't anyone raise the alarm bells about Friehling's tiny one-accountant firm auditing Madoff's multi-billion dollar hedge fund? In retrospect, we see that many people were suspicious over the years, but whenever suspicions were raised to the SEC and other authorities, no one paid much attention.

Given all the blatant red flags and the incestuous

rotation of players between the regulated and the regulators, one has to wonder how many other massive frauds are in play right now.

Post-Madoff

Madoff's $65 billion fraud earned him the maximum allowable prison sentence. One hundred and fifty years should give him ample time to think about all the people he wronged. Of course, anyone who defrauds so many people over several decades is unlikely to regret anything other than his capture.

Madoff's victims certainly have regrets, and it is truly tragic to see the devastation one selfish person has unleashed upon so many unsuspecting victims. One hundred and fifty years will never give these people back the retirement funds, the savings, or the rest of the money they have lost. Nor will his sentence help restore their faith in humanity.

Some might argue that the investors should have seen the warning signs. However, despite the numerous red flags, hindsight is always twenty-twenty. Some victims relied upon professional financial advisors for advice. Others, swept up in the success of friends and relatives, were eager to get an inside track on the stellar returns.

Those investing in feeder funds that fed into Madoff's ultimate Ponzi scheme generally had little or no information on the underlying investment. A one-line investment may have identified Madoff's fund as a holding, but provided no further information on the assets contained within it. Aside from the lack of transparency, many did not have the financial acumen to ask the right questions. Still others looked at historical returns and assumed that not only were they real, but that the same track record would continue in the future. This illustrates perhaps the best lesson for us all; never invest in something you don't understand. The only person ultimately accountable for your own well-being—financial, emotional and otherwise—is you.

CHAPTER 15

PONZI AND PYRAMID SCHEMES

EOPLE USE THE TERMS PONZI schemes and pyramid schemes interchangeably to describe frauds that pay early investors with money contributed by later investors. Both schemes share common traits like generous returns and quick payouts. Are they really the exactly same thing?

They are not. There are striking similarities, however. Under both schemes, initial investors often make enormous profits, just as we have seen with the Ponzi schemes in this book.

Early Ponzi scheme victims get good payouts, both as an enticement to invest more funds, and to snare more investors as they tell their friends. Early pyramid scheme entrants also have better odds that the people entering the scheme after them will pay up. The fact that it is a pyramid scheme is still unknown. There are many potential contributors to recruit and the market is untapped.

Perhaps the most striking similarity in both schemes is that there is no underlying investment. They are also similar in the sense that the so-called profits never last very long. These artificial returns are ill-gotten gains and can only continue as long as new investors join the scheme.

Another common trait both schemes share is the presence of some foreign or complicated element. The concept is presented, but underlying details are never fully explained. If further background was provided, it would become clear that there was no meaningful business behind the scheme.

Both are marketed with a sense of urgency and often incorporate a time-limited offer. For a Ponzi scheme, this is portrayed as a once-in-a-lifetime investment opportunity. In a pyramid scheme, it is typically promoted as "getting in on the ground floor" for greater certainty of payout.

While there are similarities, there are also some key differences.

The most fundamental difference between a Ponzi scheme and a pyramid scheme is to whom you pay your money. Under a Ponzi scheme, you pay the fraudster directly. Often it is portrayed as an investment in the Ponzi schemer's business, or as the investor providing a loan to finance something, like inventory. In a pyramid scheme, you give your money to the investors before you. The earliest contributors to the scheme are usually the only ones who make any money.

In a pyramid scheme, each participant only has access to a limited amount of the scheme's money, since he only gets the payout from people who invest after he does. In a Ponzi scheme, the fraudster has access to all of the money.

Pyramid schemes require everyone to be actively involved in recruitment. The participants are acutely aware that without the momentum of new investors, the whole thing will collapse. Payments to people at the top of the pyramid depend upon getting new peoples' money in at the bottom.

This self-recruitment is not normally part of a Ponzi scheme, but it is the most easily recognizable hallmark of a pyramid scheme. While those entering a pyramid scheme may understand how it pays out, they are unlikely to know whether they are entering at the pyramid base, or at a later stage, when there is a greater risk of the money flow grinding to a halt.

The person starting the pyramid might also list "sham" contributors to make it appear there are more people contributing than is really the case. In this way, he keeps more of the incoming funds, since the next level of contributors pay the person above them.

Passive vs. Active Involvement

For ease of reference, we will call contributors in either scheme "investors", only because that is how the contributors often label themselves. We use the term investor very loosely, since it is painfully obvious that neither the Ponzi nor the pyramid scheme are anything close to legitimate investments.

Strangely enough, most pyramid investors know a collapse is inevitable at some point. Like children playing *musical chairs,* there is a very real fear that they will not get a seat when the music stops. However, because they are actively bringing new investors in, they feel a false sense of control. They are certain they can both recruit enough people to ensure their own payout and foresee the eventual implosion in order to jump out ahead of a collapse. Of course, rarely do people play the game for a short enough time, and most will lose their money.

Contrast this with a Ponzi scheme, where the investor hands over his money with no active involvement afterward. Naturally, the Ponzi investor assumes his investment is both passive and legitimate. In other words, he incorrectly assumes his money is under professional management. As we know, nothing could be further from the truth.

Sense of Urgency

In a Ponzi scheme, only the fraudster feels a sense of urgency after the original investment. Ponzi scheme investors believe their money is in a bona fide investment that they plan to hold for a long time. They believe their only risk exposure is overall market fluctuations. Contrast this with a pyramid scheme, where all the contributors feel a need to act quickly. They know that without new money, the scheme will collapse and they will lose their money. They must remain highly motivated to recruit new contributors to the pyramid or they won't get paid.

Perception of Legitimacy

Pyramid scheme investors often sense that what they are investing in might be illegal. Even so, the promise of such lucrative returns lends an air of excitement. On some level, they worry it is too good to be true, but don't want to miss out on the action.

They know that most pyramid schemes will fail to make money at best and lose all their money at worst. Yet they assume they are contributing at the

Ponzi and Pyramid Schemes

right time, so it is worth the gamble. To many people it is like buying a lottery ticket. Both schemes play on our sense of greed.

Investment Size and Number of Investors

Since pyramid schemes typically involve smaller amounts of money than Ponzi schemes, many more investors are required. Each person must recruit many people below themselves for a chance of a payout. Small investments from many people indicate a potential pyramid scheme.

A smaller investment also means that not only are pyramid scheme participants less likely to investigate the details upfront, they are also less likely to pursue legal action when the gambit ultimately fails to pay off.

Investment Horizon

The investment horizon or payback time represents the amount of time between investment and redemption. Typically, the time horizon with a pyramid scheme is very short, often weeks. A few of the most successful pyramid schemes in history have lasted 12 to 18 months, which is unusually long. A pyramid scheme's continued operation requires the constant recruitment of large numbers of people by many others, so it does not take long for something to fail. A pyramid scheme is like a chain letter—one pause and the pyramid collapses.

Ponzi schemes tend to last longer, often years or decades. There are fewer investors, each usually contributing much larger amounts than in a pyramid scheme. The large sum of money in a Ponzi scheme in itself provides stability and staying power. All the amounts are controlled and manipulated by the Ponzi schemer, who will of course do everything he can to stretch the time horizon. By convincing you to roll over your investment, he can manage cash levels effectively.

Affinity

Ponzi schemes and pyramid schemes both rely on affinity, just in different ways. Ponzi schemes target like groups of people, affiliated by common association. It could be religion, nationality, or political beliefs. The European Kings Club Ponzi used a conspiracy theory as a common theme—us against them. We trust people like ourselves. We might also feel akin to people on our side when facing a common adversary.

Pyramid schemes rely on affinity with a twist. Because the investor is required to recruit a multitude of new members, he naturally approaches friends and family. Word of mouth implies trust. There are no better salespeople than those you know and trust. Since we tend to associate with people most like ourselves, the end result is a natural affinity. This is why people involved in a pyramid scheme tend to originate from the same background.

Since a pyramid scheme requires so many more people, it will also spread like wildfire. You will likely hear about it simultaneously from multiple sources. If your 80 year-old grandmother is feverishly recruiting her fellow parishioners at church, it could be a pyramid scheme. If you hear about an opportunity to strike it rich from several different people in your social circle, it might be a pyramid scheme. If they all urge you to contribute—and fast, before it collapses—then it is definitely a pyramid scheme.

Perhaps you hear stories of fantastical returns—only the success story is a friend of a friend, never someone you can independently verify. Such an unprovable claim almost always points to a pyramid scheme.

Aftermath

Once a fraud is uncovered, funds are frozen and a proper accounting is necessary to unwind each transaction and determine the ownership and division of any remaining money. This can be complicated, given that the true nature of the scheme was misrepresented from the start.

Forensic accountants can trace back each transaction and restate them to reflect the true nature of the scheme, and determine how to divide any recovered funds. Since the claimed investments were never made, any "profits" were merely redistributions from one investor to another. These need to be unwound to give everyone back their money, or at least a proportionate share of what is left.

This unwinding is usually only done for larger Ponzi schemes, since they typically involve significant amounts of money per investor. Since pyramid schemes rely on a much higher number of contributors with smaller amounts per person, it is not feasible or even possible to trace back the source of funds to each person.

The end result is the same under both schemes.

Almost all contributors are equally out of pocket, not only from the fraud of the Ponzi or pyramid scheme, but also because of legal expenses to recover the stolen funds.

The Securities and Exchange Commission characterized Burks' Rex Venture Group and ZeekRewards as a combined Ponzi and pyramid scheme.

While new investors paid their money to ZeekRewards, thousands of them actively advertised for new recruits. They earned points for new recruits, which could ultimately be converted into cash. Thus, Burks' points scheme was a thinly disguised pyramid scheme, with the points equivalent to the cash contributions. However, the key difference that made it a Ponzi scheme was that all the money was under his control. Anyone wanting to redeem points had to go through him. As in other Ponzi schemes, the actual earnings were much smaller in magnitude than what Burks claimed, so there was never enough cash to convert outstanding points into cash.

Burks' scheme ultimately failed when too many people wanted to convert their points into cash. There was not enough cash to back the claims.

The SEC alleged that he sold securities in violation of federal securities laws in a civil claim. In August 2012, Burks pleaded no contest and turned his company, Rex Ventures, over to a receiver. He paid a $4 million civil penalty (what was left in his possession) and ceased operations. While he has not been criminally charged, the SEC investigation is still active.

Pyramid schemes, like Ponzi schemes, are illegal

in many countries, including the United States, United Kingdom, and Canada. Usually once a large-scale fraud of this type takes place, countries pass laws to render it illegal. Pyramid schemes are still legal in many countries, simply because this swindle has not occurred on a wide enough scale to develop laws to prevent it. Sadly, laws are often enacted after the fact, and only after inflicting widespread harm to many people.

Famous Pyramid Schemes

Several of the largest pyramid schemes occurred in Eastern Europe after the fall of communism. People were poverty-stricken but optimistic about their newfound freedom. Having never experienced free-market economies, they did not see anything amiss with the outsized returns promised them.

One of the largest pyramid schemes took place in Albania in 1997. The tiny European nation covers less than 30,000 square kilometers and is home to less than three million people. It is hardly the place you expect to find rampant fraud. However, if the conditions are right, certain people use those conditions to their advantage, and a country newly emerged from communism is an easy target. A multitude of pyramid schemes took the country by storm in the 1990s, causing strife and ruin.

The early to mid 1990s were a time of great social and economic upheaval in Albania. The communist dictatorship of Enver Hoxha had toppled after almost fifty years of rule from 1944 to 1992. Like Russia, Albania transitioned to a free market economy but not easily. The country was impoverished, lacked financial and legal infrastructure, and had no exposure to capitalism. In other words, it was the perfect environment to unleash one of the biggest pyramid schemes to date on an unsuspecting population.

The first scheme occurred in 1991, run by a former government official. At the peak of the pyramid scheme explosion, fully two-thirds of Albanians had invested in one or more of the schemes. By 1997, the schemes crashed so profoundly that the Albanian Rebellion of 1997 also became known by another name—the Pyramid Crisis. Though the population of Albania was a mere three million people, total losses were estimated at over $1.2 billion. That is a staggering amount of money to remove from the economy of an impoverished country.

The pyramid collapse plunged the nation into full-fledged revolt and chaos. Albanians suspected government involvement in the schemes and staged violent demonstrations in the streets. Before United Nations troops moved in, more than two thousand people had died in the uprising. The country's finances also collapsed. At least twenty-five pyramid schemes collapsed in 1997 alone.

Albania wasn't the only country where widespread fraud of this type occurred. It has happened in Russia, Romania, Bulgaria, and Serbia. Nearly every country transitioning from communism to a free market economy has seen huge losses in these schemes.

Countries in transition from communism often lack regulatory bodies. The economy was previously tightly controlled by the state, and there were no capital markets. The new market economy lacks the rules and controls for adequate oversight. They also might also lack laws specifically outlawing pyramid schemes, so there would be no repercussions to the organizers.

A transition to a free market economy also often involves economic hardship. The country's currency might have been artificially pegged to another currency, and many economic staples are subsidized. As the country moves to a free market economy, the currency could devalue, often substantially. Much of the population lives in poverty, so a get-rich-quick promise of a pyramid scheme is very enticing.

Lastly, citizens in these countries have had limited or no exposure to capitalism. Never having had their own money to invest in business opportunities, they often fail to recognize that the advertised rewards are unlikely to materialize. What seems inconceivable to many people in free market economies seems possible to those getting their first taste of capitalism. When they are bombarded with images of vacations and luxury goods, they take the outrageous promises at face value.

CHAPTER 16

FLEECED IN FLORIDA

C HARLES PONZI SOLD FLORIDA SWAMPLAND to unsuspecting investors under the name *Charpon* (derived from his first and last name) after his release from prison. While people no longer fall for the old Florida swampland ruse, they still fall prey to other types of fraud. Florida seems to be a destination of choice for fraudsters, and Ponzi schemes occur more frequently here than in any other state. Is there something in the water? Are Floridians more gullible?

No they are not. Yet Florida boasts more frauds per capita than anywhere else in the United States. Florida may not be a global financial capital like New York or London, but it has the same securities laws, regulatory reporting and oversight as anywhere else. So why does fraud seem more prevalent in Florida compared to anywhere else in the United States?

While few financial and investment companies are based in Florida, plenty of money-saving people are. Florida is home to more retirees per capita than anywhere else in North America, and many of them are affluent. Fraudsters don't necessarily target the wealthiest people, but instead focus their efforts on those who plan to invest their money for a long time. In addition to a significant number of the gray-haired set, there are also several large ethnic groups in Florida who are easy targets for affinity fraud. Florida is truly a Ponzi schemer's paradise.

The last reason we hear of so many Ponzi schemes in Florida is simply that it is the fourth most populous state after California, Texas, and New York.

Too Good to be True

Scott Rothstein operated in Miami, as did Nevin Shapiro. The Madoff's kept a home in Palm Beach, where they were active in the south Florida social scene. There they enticed friends in their social circle to invest. Allen Stanford found many investors in South Florida as well. Three of the biggest Ponzi schemes of all time fleeced Florida investors.

Copy-Cat Frauds

There have been many other smaller frauds in Florida as well, if you consider hundreds of millions of dollars "small." I will highlight some of the more interesting ones here. Many are copycat schemes, strikingly similar to the top ten Ponzi schemes, only on a smaller scale. When you dissect the details, most Ponzi schemes are simply variations of a few tried-and-true, time-tested frauds.

At seventy-five years old, Kenneth Thenan appeared to share a similar background with many of the affluent Florida retirees he targeted. To attract money, he knew he needed to appear successful, so his wealthy appearance was part of the scam. Thenan managed to bilk investors out of $300 million with a grocery-trading scheme in the 1990s, about the time Nevin Shapiro was engaged in his grocery diverting scam. Baseball star Joe DiMaggio was among the 1,800 people who fell for Thenan's scam. He promised returns of 40%.

Louis Felipe Perez offered "no risk loans" in his jewelry business, similar to Petters' consumer electronics scam. Instead of non-existent electronics, he sold $40 million in promissory notes to finance fake diamonds.

Like Charles Ponzi's swampland scam, real estate swindles are ever popular. In early 2013, Cay Club Resorts and Marinas duped 1,400 investors out of $300 million, promising a guaranteed 15% through rental units at resort properties. The company executives paid themselves instead. They diverted $30 million in fees and commissions in addition to using investor funds for personal purchases of boats and airplanes.

According to the SEC, Fred Davis Clark, Jr., president of Cay Club Resorts and Marinas, started the company in 2004 with David W. Schwarz, chief accounting officer and three others. As finances deteriorated, they misrepresented the financial status of the company to lure new investor money. The supposed rental income paid to investors came from new investors to the scheme.

Gaston Cantens, a Miami real estate developer and president of Royal West Properties, Inc., defrauded investors of $135 million in another real estate scheme. His affinity fraud targeted Cuban-American investors with the promise of risk-free returns of 9%-16% by investing in mortgage-backed promissory notes. His five-year sentence was little consolation to his many investors, who lost most of their money.

In another affinity fraud, Haitian Americans were cheated out of more than $23 million by George L. Theodule and Creative Capital. Theodule claimed a guaranteed return of 100% within 90 days with his stock and option trading methods. He also claimed that trading profits were used to fund new business ventures, which benefited the Haitian community in both Florida and Haiti. Instead, he lost the money stock trading, and diverted much of the remainder for his personal use.

Other variations of affinity fraud have included the gay community and various religious groups.

Two brothers with different last names, Joel Steinger and Steven Steiner, bilked 29,000 investors out of $837 million with a discounted life-insurance scheme. Through their company, Mutual Benefits Corporation, they claimed money could be made buying life insurance policies at a discount.

The investors bought the fractional units of life insurance policies at a discount and then supposedly received the face value of the life insurance policy when the insured person died. The brothers claimed the policies insured elderly or terminally ill people. In fact, the premiums paid by new investors were simply paid to earlier investors. They funneled money to themselves under the guise of "consulting fees."

Born and Raised

Perhaps another reason why Florida has more Ponzi schemes is the transient nature of the population. Many people are seasonal residents, and a significant portion of the permanent residents moved to Florida later in life. Perhaps no one expects a multi-decade track record from an investment advisor, since they haven't been there for decades themselves.

Criminals can reinvent themselves here, and very few people will know they have fabricated the facts. Add in a time-limited opportunity, and many people do not spend the time required for adequate due diligence.

Conclusion

A fraudster thinks of himself first. His goal is to steal the most money he can with the least effort. Whether he operates in a retirement community in Florida or finds his victims indirectly through feeder funds does not matter in the end. What does matter is how you react to his pitch.

Whether you live in Florida, Missouri, or a country transitioning to a free market economy, the best way to protect yourself is to educate yourself as much as possible about your potential investment. Get independent advice for anything you do not understand, and resist the pressure to invest in a hurry. A truly good investment will still be a good investment tomorrow.

Finally, if you are suspicious, alert the authorities right away. While you have no control over when and how they act, at least you will put questionable investments and characters on the radar. Let the authorities decide whether the investment is legitimate or not. Many prospective victims will thank you.

CHAPTER 17

PONZI-SPOTTING

PONZI-SPOTTING IS LIKE BEING ON a big game safari. You can drive through the middle of the Serengeti and miss animals hiding in plain sight. Like a leopard stalking his next meal, a predator lies in wait for his next victim. A fraudster sees you coming, even if you cannot see him. He notes your weaknesses as he moves in for the kill. He will trick you into doing exactly the opposite of what you would normally do.

A scammer will promise you a dream, a chance of a lifetime to enrich yourself, and banish all your financial worries. At first, you are skeptical. So was almost every one of his earlier victims. But, you wonder—*what if you could* make all that money? Do you really want to miss an opportunity of a lifetime? Or could the promise simply be too good to be true?

One by one, the scam artist answers your questions, brushes away your doubts, and hooks you. Be fooled, and his empty promises will ruin you.

Hunters always gain the initial advantage when they spot their prey before the prey spots them. You may be nothing but prey in the eyes of a Ponzi schemer, but on the other hand, you are far from powerless.

You can fight back. With a good guide, you can easily spot Ponzi red flags. Listen to your intuition. If it sounds too good to be true, it usually is.

Easy money is the most tempting money around. Especially if you have been pinching pennies and doing without. Scoring big on an investment not only increases your bank balance, it instills a feeling of pride. Even if it sounds too good to be true, a scam artist knows how to counter your objections, one by one. There are time-tested methods scam artists use to convince you to ignore your instincts.

Penny Wise, Ponzi Foolish

Ponzi schemes can exist and thrive, even in a less than ideal environment. Their promises of outsized investment returns become even more attractive in times of low interest rates and underperforming markets.

We can expose them by simply knowing what to look for. Aside from our personal finances, think of how society as a whole would benefit if we could uncover and prevent a higher percentage of these crimes.

Preventing these schemes would redirect the billions spent frivolously by Ponzi schemers on sports cars and mansions. Instead, the money would stay in the hands of the people who worked decades to earn it. People financially ruined by these fraudulent schemes would have savings instead of depending on social assistance or the goodwill of relatives. People with adequate savings often donate to charity. They pay taxes that directly and indirectly help low-income seniors, fund health care, or improve our overall standard of living.

Ponzi-Spotting

Less money would be required to fund investor restitution or investigate and prosecute fraudsters. Every dollar taken by a fraudster is a dollar removed from many people's pockets. This concentration of wealth in a Ponzi schemer's hands causes further damage to our collective well-being.

The sheer magnitude of Ponzi schemes and fraud in general makes it difficult for government and law enforcement to identify and expose them. They simply do not have enough resources to detect every scam. When you add confusion over overlapping state and federal jurisdictions, coupled with potential conflicts of interest between the regulators and the regulated, it is clear that we do not have a clear line of sight. To be effective, we need to employ a different approach.

The more we can educate people about fraud, the better chance we all have of exposing fraudsters as quickly as possible. A well-informed investor is a protected investor. They are much less likely to succumb to the scam.

Most important of all is to report our suspicions. Let the authorities determine whether the investment is legitimate or not. (see resources listed at the end of this book). The secretive nature of these investment schemes allows criminals to carry on without being prosecuted. They repeatedly replicate the same scheme on a new group of victims. Awareness and a healthy dose of skepticism make for a very good start when evaluating any investment. Before making any decisions, ask yourself these fundamental questions:

- Q: Why doesn't anyone else offer this rate of return for a similar investment?

- A: Because they can't. It is not real.

- Q: Why do I have to invest today? If this is such a great investment, why can't I wait a few days, weeks or months?

- A: While timing can and does have an impact on investment returns, a good investment will stand the test of time and still provide attractive returns. There is always enough time to research your decision before acting on it.

- Q: If you can only get in today, what does that say about your investment return for tomorrow and the day after?

- A: It means the investment is not viable. The promoter will not be able to sell you a worthless investment tomorrow.

- Q: Is the investment regulated? Does it have a prospectus? Investments governed by a regulatory body are subject to statutory rules and reporting. Most investments in developed countries are governed by a regulatory body

- A: If the promoter cannot answer these questions or does not offer a prospectus, run away. Most legitimate investments require prospectuses disclosing financial and risk details about the underlying investment. If this information is not provided, it is likely illegal and a scam.

While these basic questions cannot always prevent you from getting duped, asking them will likely deter a criminal. At the very least, it leaves him scrambling for excuses, and possibly a quick exit. If it is a good investment, there is always enough time to invest after doing a bit of research.

In hindsight, many Ponzi scheme victims had initial misgivings about their investments. Unfortunately, they were ultimately enticed by the generous investment returns. Don't be tempted and become the next victim.

Bernard Madoff managed to run his fraud for so many years because his investors reinvested for years, even decades. If not for the 2008 financial crisis, which forced many of his large investors to redeem their investments, his Ponzi scheme would probably still be running today. His scheme is also proof that anyone can fall for a Ponzi scheme. Many of his investors were financially sophisticated: business tycoons, charitable foundations and even other hedge funds. Madoff's fraud was far-reaching partly because he invested other hedge funds' money in his fund, as a fund-of funds investment. It widened the scope of his reach, but also kept him a step away from the prying eyes of authorities.

If you do ever uncover suspicious activity, do not sign the check, and take your money elsewhere. Equally important is to report your suspicions to the authorities. This could be the securities commission in your country, or local law enforcement.

While the following red flags alone do not confirm a fraudulent investment, they should stop you in your tracks. At the very least, you should do considerably more research and background checks on both the investment and the person offering it. Most or all of the red flags were present in each of the Ponzi schemes in this book.

PONZI RED FLAGS

Unusually high returns with little or no risk

Risk and potential return are highly correlated. Higher returns usually mean exposing yourself to additional risk. In addition to higher returns, risk also increases the likelihood of loss. For this increased risk, an investor generally expects a higher return over the long term. The difference in return between a high-risk investment and a low-risk investment is known as the risk premium.

For example, government treasury bills (T-bills) are offered at what is considered the "risk-free" rate. This is because a stable government can generally be relied upon to honor their debt (or pay the notes when due). Many investors are willing to lend the government money. Therefore, the government does not need to add a premium return to entice investors. Of course, this means the investment provides low returns, since the risk of default is low.

A company selling stock or debt usually has a rate of return above the T-bill rate, which represents the "risk-free" rate plus a risk premium, which varies according to the company's creditworthiness and credit rating. A company has a greater probability of bankruptcy than a country. All things being equal, an investor will want a higher return than the risk-free rate to compensate for this additional risk.

While the world abounds with many investment opportunities, they are not endless. As investors compete for a limited number of investments, supply and demand level the playing field so that investments with a similar risk profile will pay similar returns. A high return with a supposed minimal risk is a waving red flag. So is any investment paying a materially higher return than similar investments in its class.

Allen Stanford offered a return several percentage points higher than the going rate for Certificates of Deposit. Why couldn't other banks replicate his strategy and offer similar returns? His claim that the Stanford International Bank invested in highly liquid financial instruments was only one of several red flags.

Consistent Returns over Long Periods

Ponzi schemers seem to have an uncanny ability to produce positive returns, year after year. History tells us that such consistency is impossible over anything other than a very short time horizon. Our global and national economies fluctuate. Wars, recessions, resource availability, government stability, and even weather patterns impact investment return. Uncertain times tend to either increase or depress resource prices, currencies and interest rates. Thus, all of the related investments will fluctuate over time also.

Bernard Madoff's double-digit returns were also

remarkable for their consistency year in and year out, over decades. This was despite several market crashes that decimated every other investment guru. Allen Stanford also provided investment returns that were unbelievably consistent. Stanford even had two years of identical 15.71% returns, statistically improbable when you consider his claim of a diversified investment portfolio.

If you are earning a 20% return per year even while global stock markets are declining, there is a very good chance your returns are fabricated. Markets rise and fall with the global economy.

Investments offering a guaranteed return, especially attractive returns over long periods, can be a fraud red flag. While you can lock in your money long-term in a guaranteed investment certificate (GIC), it is typically at a very low rate, since the lender or seller must assume the risk of continuing to pay you far into the future despite economic changes. The longer the term, the less likely anyone can predict the future with any certainty.

The most successful investors cannot beat the market over the long term. They are simply unable to predict future events with great certainty. In fact, most successful investors profit from investments with lower but steady returns and low volatility. A consistent return over time usually results in a higher overall profit.

If an investment is offered at a fixed rate, the company offering it must deduct some portion of that expected return as insurance to compensate against unforeseen events. In addition, their fees must come off the top. Although their average long-term return might be stellar, it will include years where they have made money, and years where they have lost money, like everyone else. Great investment managers just lose less, or less often.

Even legendary investors like Warren Buffet and George Soros have the occasional bad year or investment loss. Ponzi schemers never do, at least not until they are caught and their scheme unravels.

Any guaranteed return, or guaranteed minimum return for an equity investment is likely to be fraudulent. Similarly, guaranteed returns for long-term promissory notes or other debt deserve close scrutiny.

Significant return in a short period of time

Another red flag on investment return is a stellar return over a very short time frame. Sarah Howe's Ladies Deposit Club not only paid a fantastic return, it also advanced three months' interest up front. Most Ponzi schemers know that this will not only hook you, but will convince you to invest even more once you get that first check. They will typically offer you a quick payback to discourage you from looking elsewhere. Grab your money and run.

Time Limited or Sense of Urgency

Hooking you quickly is more critical to the scammer than ever before, now that so much information is available on the Internet. You might discover his earlier scams, or arouse suspicion with friends and family. He needs to limit the amount of research you can do before you hand over your money.

His success depends on your impulse decisions. Urgency is the number one fraud red flag. More time to think means a greater possibility of the scam being exposed.

Unregistered Investments

Most countries regulate investments. The Securities and Exchange Commission provides oversight in the United States, and similar regulatory organizations provide the same service in other countries. The investment firm and/or its representative must be registered, and cannot offer securities for sale without a prospectus. The prospectus is a very important document because it discloses the nature of the investment, important details, and related risks. Never invest without checking to see what documentation is required in your jurisdiction, and whether the materials provided meet these requirements.

Only investments considered securities require a prospectus. Unregistered investments are generally limited to debt instruments. These fall outside the scope, scrutiny or protection of securities regulators, which of course is exactly what a Ponzi operator wants.

Fraudsters often evade regulatory scrutiny by misrepresenting their supposed investment as debt. The investment is typically described as a promissory note, yet the investment returns will be derived from a source other than the debt itself. The Madoff accounting firm, Avellino and Bienes, claimed the returns were from the stock market. Alternatively, the investment profit may come from reselling a product where the investor shares in the profits, such as

Marc Dreier's grocery diverting scheme. Investments of this nature are considered securities, not debt.

As you can imagine from the above, it can be difficult for a non-expert to determine if an investment requires a prospectus or not. If you do not have the financial sophistication to easily determine this, do not invest. Do not trust or rely on the advice of a financial advisor, and don't feel stupid about not understanding it either. Remember that one of the most common tricks a fraudster employs is by describing the investment in complex terms. At best, the investment is too complex for you to monitor. At worst, it is outright fraud.

The SEC and other oversight organizations have a wealth of information to assist you. Ask yourself—why is this investment unregistered? What are they trying to hide?

Unlicensed sellers

Most Ponzi schemes involve unlicensed sellers, simply because they need to stay under the radar to perpetuate their scheme. Investment professionals typically have to abide by a code of ethics and other regulations to remain in good standing. Licensing and requirements vary by jurisdiction; your national securities regulator will have details on how you can verify this. There are also resources listed at the end of this book.

Complex strategies

If an investment cannot be explained well enough for you to understand it, do not buy it. At best, it is meant for a more sophisticated investor. At worst, and far more likely, the seller is trying to hide the true nature of the investment because it is a fraud. Never invest in something you don't understand.

Fraudsters often describe complex strategies involving derivatives, insurance, or reselling. They may present themselves as experts in an obscure area. Paul Burks' ZeekRewards and underlying penny auction business was based on a complicated system of points and referrals.

The more fraudulent the investment, the more complicated it will appear. The fraudster prevents you from discovering facts by layering on complicated methodology and terminology. He specifically attempts to make you feel too stupid to ask questions.

Foreign-Based

A foreign-based theme might or might not be present. It is closely related to the complex structure above, designed to seem legitimate, yet with enough unknowns in the foreign element that you cannot easily verify it. The country's laws are foreign to you and the language likely is too. You are unable to do your own research. You simply must trust your investment advisor. This is not a sound investment strategy.

Charles Ponzi's postal reply coupon scheme had a foreign aspect that was difficult to validate. Until the U.S. Postal Service indicated that the number of postal reply coupons in existence was a fraction of that needed for Ponzi's scheme, no one questioned it.

Secrecy

Some fraudsters will insist on secrecy, either from you in terms of what you are agreeing to, or else about the nature of the investment itself. Sarah Howe's Ladies Deposit investors were sworn to secrecy as a condition of investing.

Scammers often say they cannot divulge their secret methods, claiming their stunning returns will diminish once discovered by others. However in the long run, there are few secrets in investing. At the very least, everything can be reverse-engineered, and you can bet that any legitimate investment earning outsized returns will be copied in short order.

Secrecy is particularly effective with seniors, who otherwise might discuss an investment with their children. When the investment finally does go sour, many investors are ashamed they fell for it. Many say nothing, leaving the scammer free to troll for new victims.

Issues with paperwork

No paperwork? Forget it.

Watch for errors or strange transactions on account statements, or lack of information when you request it. Errors can indicate that the statements are manually prepared and fabricated. Excuses and delays mean there are problems. Some funds provide no reporting whatsoever. Bernard Madoff's fund was a perfect example of this.

Difficulty Getting Payment

If you are experiencing difficulty with redemptions,

it could already be too late to recover your money. The Ponzi scheme may be about to collapse.

Most Ponzi schemes will make less than a dozen payments before they stop entirely. That's just enough time to convince most investors to invest and is also enough proof for many to convince a wider circle of friends and family to invest as well.

Redemptions should also be immediate. Many investors find that redemption terms suddenly change to requiring advance notice where none was required before. Investment redemptions may not pose a problem in the early days of the scheme, but will be problematic later on when the fraudster is no longer flush with cash.

Sometimes redemptions can take a few days, in the case of very illiquid investments or large redemptions. This is normal if underlying assets must be sold in order to return funds. But never longer. Being "talked out" of a redemption, or promised even higher returns is not a legitimate practice.

Especially worrisome is the promise of still higher returns if you roll over your investment. Remember, redemptions create cash flow problems for the fraudster. The promise of higher returns and the threat of not being allowed to reinvest after redemption are classic Ponzi ploys.

Finally, investment funds must be segregated from other funds held by the seller. If you do get your money, but the check is written from a personal or an account other than where you invested, call the authorities. Commingling of investment funds with general business or personal funds is another red flag.

Exclusivity

Exclusivity is designed to make you feel indebted to the fraudster. You feel privileged for the opportunity to strike it rich—not to mention important when told you can get your friends in on the action too.

You are less likely to say no when you get the "inside track" on a surefire winner. After all, the ultra-successful investor has done you a favor by taking you under his wing. Your financial future suddenly brightens with this favor. How can you say no?

Reciprocity

An opportunity to invest alongside a millionaire also feels like a gift. The prospective investor feels a sense of reciprocity, or wanting to return a favor, which compels them to act. It is ingrained in our psyches to feel grateful to those who give us something for nothing. In turn, the Ponzi victim is likely to make allowances for their supposed benefactor. It quashes any suspicions that someone so nice would take advantage of you.

Bernard Madoff cultivated a sense of exclusivity by only allowing investors through intermediaries, and even then, only by referral. He usually rejected them the first time as well. He didn't need your money, and if he let you into his fund he was doing you a favor. Not only did this create buzz, but it also helped him stay under the radar for a long time.

Affinity

Some of the biggest scams in history have been based on affinity. Martin Sigilitto, an Anglican bishop and attorney based in St. Louis, perpetrated a Ponzi scheme starting in 2000 that he ran undiscovered for more than ten years. He took investor money and claimed to invest it in the British Lending Program with returns of 10% to 48% for one-year terms. He alleged the fund provided loans to a British real estate developer who was able to make such high returns by spotting undervalued properties and flipping them. In hindsight, the obvious questions are why the developer would not simply go to a British bank since the properties would be collateral.

Sigilitto claimed to have the inside track on this opportunity due to his expertise in international law, and said he was a lecturer at Oxford. Had anyone tried to verify his claim, they could have easily found it was a lie. Sigilitto's foreign-based investment was a fraud red flag, but his scheme remained undetected until his suspicious assistant turned him in.

Aside from the investment itself, there are additional red flags you can look for in the organization offering the investment.

Junior or Unqualified People in Senior Positions

The overwhelming majority of large-scale Ponzi schemes require more than one person to fabricate statements, fake analysis, and keep track of all the deception. While a scammer will often keep the paperwork to himself as much as possible, it becomes impossible to hide everything behind closed doors as the fraud grows. Even with the scam limited to a trusted inner circle, a large Ponzi scheme requires many people to keep things running.

Often the individuals the fraudster chooses are

young people with little or no work experience, or
people lacking senior level experience.

Several job applicants and past employees at
Stanford International Bank mentioned the lack
of qualified people. Perhaps Stanford thought he
could hide the true nature of his scheme from less-
experienced employees. Perhaps more experienced
professionals were suspicious and therefore not
willing to work there.

Sometimes rather than young employees, the
scammer has long-term employees with no formal
qualifications. People without formal qualifications
might have limited career options. Those limited
options might include working for a fraudster.

Family Employees

Scammers also often employ family. Of course, many
reputable firms do as well. The difference is usually
the degree to which family members are employed, as
well as their relative levels of responsibility. Bernard
Madoff's niece was employed straight out of university
in a senior compliance position at his firm. I am not
aware of any multi-billion dollar hedge funds that
entrust such an important position to newly minted
university grads with limited work experience.

This does not necessarily mean that the relatives are
in on the scam. What it does mean is that they might
not have the knowledge or experience necessary to
spot the wrongdoing. They are certainly less likely to
question any suspicious activities, given the complex
nature of their relationship as both an employee and
a relative of their employer.

Shady Accountants

Accountants are a key part of any successful Ponzi scheme, simply because any competent accountant would see through a Ponzi scheme in short order. This is the case whether they are accountants within the firm preparing financial statements and analysis, or external auditors signing off on the financial results. It is simply impossible to record or analyze the underlying transactions in any level of detail without uncovering the scheme. Therefore any accountant involved is likely complicit in the scheme.

Within the Ponzi schemer's organization, recordkeeping usually requires maintaining two sets of books. Accountants know how to record transactions to pass the scrutiny of regulatory audits without raising suspicions. To keep the fraud going long-term, the accountants must reconcile the real cash with what they are reporting, so that they know how much (or how little) they can afford to pay out to investors without the fund going bust. As you can imagine, it all gets quite complicated and difficult to manage.

Most qualified accountants will not risk a lucrative career to engage in fraud. Instead, the fraudster typically uses unqualified accountants, who will have some experience but lack the necessary certifications and credentials. These uncertified accountants have much more limited career options available to them, and the Ponzi scheme pay is typically more than they could earn elsewhere. With such incentives to keep their mouths shut, they might play an even more active role if the compensation is right.

Most Ponzi schemes, or any scam, for that matter, will utilize second-tier accounting firms for their external audits. Both Stanford and Madoff used tiny accounting firms that simply rubber-stamped the financial statements instead of performing audits. Multi-billion dollar organizations would require at least a dozen accountants for an audit, yet both of these firms had only one practicing accountant.

Legitimate accounting firms and accountants generally have too much to lose by participating in, or turning a blind eye to, illegal schemes. Non-certified accountants, however, have very little to lose. They will simply close up shop and disappear.

All Ponzi schemes will have most or all of these fraud red flags. Reputable investment firms will not object to further questions, and legitimate opportunities will still be around days, weeks or years later.

If you do happen to miss an opportunity, there will be plenty of others. If you think about it, no one investment should outperform others by a mile, since they all invest in the same limited universe of opportunities. Trust your research and intuition. Anything that seems too good to be true most often is.

CHAPTER 18

FRAUD DETECTION

The Tip of the Iceberg

V ERY LITTLE FRAUD IS BOTH detected and prosecuted. To understand the global magnitude of the fraud landscape, we need to look at the fraud universe as described in The Accountant's Guide to Fraud Detection and Control (Davia, Coggins, et al.). While the book's analysis refers to all types of fraud, the three main categories of fraud it mentions hold true for Ponzi schemes also:

1. Fraud identified and prosecuted—20%

2. Fraud detected but not prosecuted—40%

3. Fraud undetected—40%

The amount of fraud actually detected and prosecuted represents only the tip of the fraud iceberg.

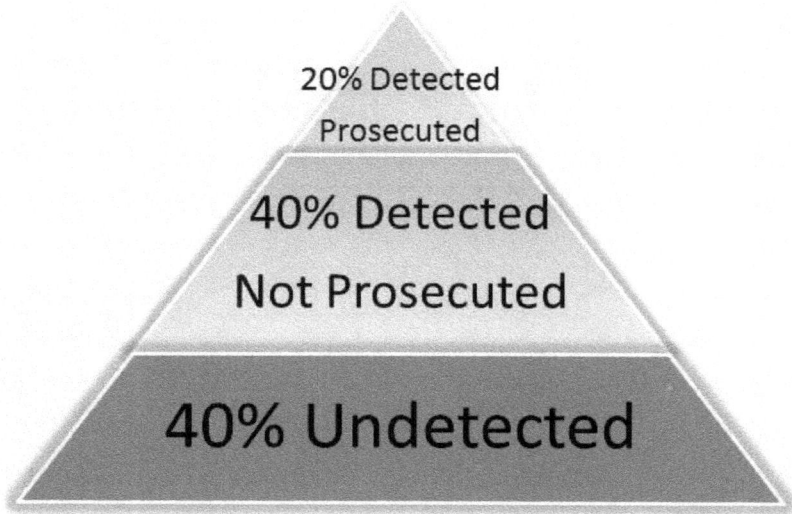

20% Detected
Prosecuted

40% Detected
Not Prosecuted

40% Undetected

80% of All Fraud is Unprosecuted

The implications are staggering when you realize that the massive frauds from the financial crisis all fit into the first category. For simplicity's sake, we will look at the top four frauds uncovered in the United States alone as a result of the 2008 financial crisis. All were over a billion dollars:

1. Madoff—$65 billion

2. Stanford—$7 billion

3. Petters—$3.7 billion

4. Rothstein—$1.4 billion

Altogether, they total over $77 billion. The 2008 United States Gross Domestic Product (GDP) was $14.2 trillion. Fraud that was actually discovered and prosecuted represents a total of 0.54% of the entire U.S. GDP. In other words, what is prosecuted is a merely a rounding error. Think about that for a moment. The United States is the largest global economy, but if we assume this same ratio applies globally, the amounts are astounding.

If we extrapolate and assume these four frauds represent only twenty percent of the total fraud out there, the real total is more than $390 billion. If this is accurate, it represents 2.7% of the entire output of the largest economy in the world.

This is a very simplistic and understated assumption since we have ignored all of the smaller Ponzi schemes discovered and prosecuted from 2008 that were less than a billion dollars. In the example above, we are only talking about Ponzi schemes and ignoring any other fraud category. A commonly held belief among fraud experts is that fraud losses of all types approximate 5% of GDP in most countries.

Based on the assumptions above, Ponzi schemes account for more than half of all fraud losses at 2.7% of GDP, since fraud losses of all types approximates 5% total of GDP. Instead of producing jobs, funding our retirements or generally improving the lives of Americans, money is repurposed to benefit the lavish lifestyles of a few fraudsters. Aside from stealing from ordinary people, scammers also shift the tax burden onto the same people, since in most cases the scam artists don't bother to pay tax on this money. There are a few notable exceptions. Tom Petters even filed fraudulent tax returns on the phantom profits he claimed his company made.

Why are Ponzi schemes so prevalent today? While recent history has exposed many, this is not the only time in history they have occurred. Of the all-time top ten, all have occurred in either the early to mid 1990s, or from 2008 to 2009. These periods shared some common elements that allowed Ponzi schemes to thrive.

Ponzi explosion

More Ponzi schemes were exposed in the mid-to-late 2000s than in recent memory. Are there really more Ponzi schemes than ever, or are we simply catching more crooks? The answer is not simple.

There are definitely more investment opportunities today than in Charles Ponzi's era almost a century ago. Our overall population is greater, and a larger proportion of affluent people have savings to invest. Our economy and financial markets are more visible and transparent with the advent of television, electronic trading, and the Internet. So we tend to hear about more of these frauds.

Better Regulation and Oversight

A definite improvement from 520 Percent Miller's day is that most investments are now regulated. But are we safer today with all this oversight?

Sadly, we are not. The world is more interconnected than ever before, which allows fraudsters to reach a very large audience. Opportunities abound, but we are also more likely to trust media and other quasi-official sources rather than doing our own research. Fraudsters also have an easier time generating fake materials. Anyone can buy a computer, a printer and related equipment. A person can fake financial statements, prospectus and instantly copy and paste numerous times.

Many of the laws designed to protect us do not apply to certain classes of investments. For example, hedge funds are directed towards "sophisticated investors" and therefore not subject to the same regulatory oversight and reporting requirements. The idea is that knowledgeable investors have the experience to know the risks of hedge fund investments. They invest at their own risk and are supposed to do their own homework.

These investors are required to meet a "means" test to prove they have enough money to afford to lose part or all of their investment. But affluence alone does not make you smart. As you can imagine, fraudsters flock to the areas with the least scrutiny.

Unregulated investments often translate into greater opportunities for fraudsters to work their schemes. Lower reporting and regulatory hurdles attract fraudsters like flies to honey.

The Investment Climate

Ponzi schemes thrive in certain environments over others. These scams seem to especially proliferate in a low interest rate environment in particular, especially when the rate drops over a short period of time. However, they can occur at any time there is a drop in financial returns, whether it be general interest rates or the stock market. While they do best in a climate of little or no regulation, they will also thrive in regulated markets, simply by skirting around the rules.

Fraudsters tend to target unsophisticated investors, who typically gravitate to fixed-rate investments (interest-bearing deposits or fixed-rate debt). They understand these types of fixed rate investments better than equity, and with locked-in rates, it seems less risky. These investors are the perfect victims. They are sold investments they do not understand, and therefore cannot validate. Ponzi schemes thrive when the following are present:

1. **Dramatic Interest Rate Declines & Historically Low Interest Rates**

   The late 1800s as well as the 1990s and 2000s all saw steep interest rate declines, and Ponzi schemes clustered around the periods when these declines were the most dramatic. All of the top ten Ponzi schemes occurred within these two periods.

   Ponzi schemes do well with sharp and recent drops in interest rates. Investors become accustomed to a certain level of return, perhaps for their income or their retirement savings plans. When lower rates result in reduced income, investors are anxious to switch into a higher yielding investment. Investors often ignore the higher risk as they chase the higher returns.

2. **Bull markets**

Investors are quick to invest when equity markets do well. This often perpetuates Ponzi schemes, since there is no shortage of new money from investors eager to get in on the action. Bull markets also result in increased media focus, which attracts additional investors. Speculation and risk-taking investments abound, as the general public moves their money to the markets to get in on the action. Bull markets tend to have a much higher proportion of unsophisticated investors. Current interest rates are almost zero after continued decreases over the last decade. Higher relative stock market yields drive more people to invest in securities overall, providing more potential capital for Ponzi schemes.

3. **Regulatory Oversight**

Hedge funds were originally restricted to sophisticated investors who understood the inherent risks and could afford to lose their investments. Given this, hedge funds have not been subject to extensive regulation. This lack of regulation and reporting transparency has not been lost on fraudsters, who often describe their investments as hedge funds. Minimal disclosure allows for easier manipulation and misleading reporting.

While hedge funds are still subject to some regulation by the SEC and other regulators, branding their schemes as hedge funds gives fraudsters a lot of leeway. It attracts the right kind of investor too. The investor must usually have a minimum net worth so they can afford to lose part or all of their investment. Recordkeeping for a few large investors is also easier for the fraudster to keep straight when his fund is simply one big lie.

While most hedge funds are not Ponzi schemes, many Ponzi schemes will be hedge funds. Fraudsters usually avoid publicly traded companies or mutual funds. Both have extensive independent oversight in the form of regulatory requirements, reporting, and independent annual audits, so discrepancies are likely to be discovered.

4. **Investment Type**

Of the Ponzi top ten, most used promissory notes with a generous guaranteed rate. Stanford was a notable exception. He started his very own bank, but modeled it on a variation of a high guaranteed return with high-yield certificates of deposits (CDs).

Petters also employed promissory notes; however, the hedge funds that invested in his promissory notes were sub-Ponzi schemes to his overall scheme.

Only Madoff described his investment as a hedge fund. While his returns were re-markably consistent, he was careful not to explicitly promise a fixed rate. Rather, he let his decades of investment performance (fictitious of course) imply a guaranteed 12% rate of return.

5. **Easy credit**

Easy credit allows investors to borrow funds to invest. The individual investor's finances become highly leveraged as he takes on more debt to fund investments. When an economic downturn occurs, it can lead to financial disaster for many, such as in the 2008 financial crisis.

6. **Technology**

The advent of the Internet has brought more information and investment opportunities than ever before. While the Internet has made everything more transparent and accessible, it has also allowed fraudsters to troll for more unwitting victims with promises of spectacular returns.

7. **Do-it-Yourself Investing**

Our changing society has resulted in less of a social safety net. In the past, employees typically worked for one employer for most of their career, and this employer in turn provided a monthly pension. Today, more employees are mobile. The employer defined benefit pension plans of yesterday have been mostly replaced with defined contribution plans, where individuals bear the risk and reward of investment performance. Instead of professional money management, their savings are self-managed, which can be disastrous when decision makers lack financial sophistication.

CHAPTER 19

COLLATERAL DAMAGE: THE VICTIMS

We All Pay the Price

THE COLLATERAL DAMAGE FROM A Ponzi scheme is much more widespread than it first appears. The obvious victims are people who invested in the scheme in the first place. They are not the only victims, however.

Society at-large pays a very high price in terms of increased regulatory costs as well as legal costs to investigate, prosecute, and jail the criminals. Whether we pay higher taxes or fees, we all end up paying the price for these criminal schemes.

Forensic accountants are usually required to trace and recover the funds, and the legal costs to investigate and prosecute are high. In addition, the fraudster will likely claim insolvency and as added insult to injury, his or her defense costs will be paid by the taxpayers.

Finally, laws and regulations are typically not developed until someone does something wrong, gets caught and inspires the new law. That adds costs to lobby for and implement new laws, regulations and regulatory watchdogs, and the ongoing cost of compliance and reporting for those regulated.

White-collar crime is today's equivalent of the bank holdup or stagecoach robbery of yesteryear. Armed holdups still occur, but today these old-school crimes net mostly small-scale criminals several thousand dollars at best.

Today's enterprising trickster is more likely to use technology and social engineering to rip people off on a much larger scale of millions or even billions of dollars. Yet we punish these crimes to a lesser degree. The perpetrator gets off lightly, often forfeiting only the investor money he has not yet spent, and possibly paying a fine. Often the bigger frauds are the only ones that result in jail time. Society considers Ponzi schemes and other white-collar crimes to be less serious, partly because the true costs are hidden.

Our justice system assigns hefty prison terms for armed robbery and rightfully so. Violent crimes must carry a penalty to ensure the criminal is deterred. Otherwise, our society will become lawless and violent.

But should we be benchmarking white-collar crime against traditional crimes like armed robbery based only on the level of physical harm? The answer is no. Both types of crime are equally damaging to individuals and society as a whole, just in different ways. Jail time and fines should reflect this.

Fraud sentences have not kept pace with technological advances. A hundred years ago, thieves could only rob one place or person at a time, and faced significant jail time if caught.

Now fraudsters can amass billions with impunity, decimating the personal wealth of thousands or even millions of people. At the very least, fraud disrupts commerce, discourages investment and decreases our overall economic well-being. At best, it adds regulatory and oversight costs that are ultimately borne by every taxpayer.

Given the impacts, why do we give such light sentences for fraud and white-collar crime? It is because white-collar crimes have evolved, but laws to counteract them lag. Laws tend to evolve only after the fact, and gradually at that. Mavrodi's Russian Ponzi scheme is one example. The laws did not yet exist to prosecute the crime. In countries where laws do exist, the sentences are still minimal. Regulations and sentences have long been in place in the United States and most other Western countries, only because Ponzi schemes have taken place in our free-market economies for almost a hundred years.

Even in the United States, a legal patchwork of regulatory oversight and enforcement exists between state and federal jurisdiction. At best, this results in delayed investigations, such as in the case of Paul Burks and ZeekRewards, or worst case, fraud that received no investigation and remains unprosecuted.

In the ZeekRewards hybrid pyramid-Ponzi case, the North Carolina Attorney General's office received numerous complaints but did not act, believing the problem was a securities issue, which would fall under the Securities and Exchange Commission and federal law. In the meantime, many more victims handed over their money before the scheme finally shut down.

With such a large payoff, a light prison sentence is no deterrent at all to a fraudster. In the last few years, the sentencing has started to evolve and now more accurately reflects the gravity of the crime for at least the larger Ponzi schemes. Madoff's and Stanford's sentences mean that they will serve out their lives in prison, but they received the maximum because their billion-dollar frauds were so widespread and highly publicized. They are the exception, not the rule. Many fraudsters still receive no jail time.

Sentencing for robbery, fraud and other crimes vary by state in the U.S., but for an average theft of $10,000 or less, the typical bank robber in Florida today serves an average sentence of just over seven years. Part of the reason for the long sentence, and rightfully so, is that bank robbery is considered a violent crime.

While there are no individual statistics for fraud or Ponzi schemes (a subset of fraud), the sentences are often much lighter, even though most crimes involve millions or even billions of dollars. Only about half of those convicted actually serve any jail time, and of those, jail time averages a mere 4 years. The others convicted receive fines, somewhat ironic as a deterrent if you consider their modus operandi for raising money.

Ponzi schemes do not abruptly terminate victims' lives with a bullet but many victims will tell you their lives effectively did end the day they lost their savings. Aside from financial ruin, many also experience serious depression, suicidal thoughts, and marriage and family breakdowns. Many fraud victims report feeling violated, and exhibit the same psychological symptoms as victims of violent crime.

Collateral Damage: The Victims

While a Ponzi schemer does not hold a gun to anyone's head, his average theft is easily in the millions, and the scale and extent of destruction is much larger than a bank robbery. Should his sentence be half or less that of someone holding up a bank?

I do not believe the sentencing for bank robberies should be lighter, but rather fraud sentences should be longer. Fraud is anything but a victimless crime, and the extent of the damage, both in emotional and economic terms should be reflected in sentencing guidelines.

Laying Blame

Society tends to blame the victim in a Ponzi scheme almost as much as the perpetrator. There is an implicit assumption that they got what they deserved because they were greedy. We think victims should have known better, or that their greed got the better of them. Until that is, it happens to us.

Many fraud victims are just like you and me. They likely had initial doubts, but one by one, their objections were eliminated by a smooth-talking con. They were careful at first, investing a small amount. When the promised returns materialized, month after month and year after year, the investment's legitimacy was validated. They invested more—often their life's savings. It really is impossible to know if we would act differently in the same situation.

Many victims simply do not come forward. They blame themselves, ashamed that they were deceived so easily. The warning signs are glaring at them in the rear view mirror. Unbeknownst to them, they were not alone, and their reticence to come forward allows the fraudster to victimize many more people.

Marriage breakdown is common. Trust issues arise, especially if one person made the investment decision, with or without their spouse's knowledge. Often the true magnitude of loss remains hidden from the unsuspecting spouse until it results in irreversible loss. Some victims report symptoms similar to post-traumatic stress disorder, depression, and even suicidal thoughts. Anxiety and insomnia are also common.

Too old to work, unable to recoup savings or get credit is a dramatic reversal of fortune from a lifetime of saving. Many describe waking each day from what they hope is a bad dream, only to rediscover their stark financial reality.

It is because society partially blames the victim that these fraudsters tend to get off easy. Only a small amount of the money is typically recovered.

Trolling for Victims

Fraudsters are indiscriminate in their choice of victims, though they often prefer to cast their net as far and as wide as possible. More fish in the sea often leads to more bites on the hook. It also means more money for them.

They often prefer middle-class people to wealthy ones. Wealthy people tend to employ professional financial advisors who pre-screen investments, and fraudsters want to avoid close scrutiny at all costs. The wealthy also have the means to litigate if problems arise.

Collateral Damage: The Victims

Many middle-class people have accumulated substantial savings over a lifetime of work. More importantly, they are less inclined to spend their hard-earned savings on legal fees until it is too late. Middle-class people are the demographic sweet spot for a Ponzi schemer.

Regardless of who they are, most Ponzi scheme victims eventually pool all their money with the Ponzi schemer because the investment returns are so spectacular.

As Charles Ponzi said, months before he died penniless in Rio de Janeiro:

> *"My business was simple. It was the old game of robbing Peter to pay Paul."*

CHAPTER 20

THE NEXT BIG PONZI—A PREDICTION

WILL THERE BE MORE PONZI schemes? Yes, without a doubt. Many are in operation right now, including the one that will eclipse Madoff's in size within the decade. It will continue on undiscovered, until a stock market correction or other financial calamity causes investors to redeem their money.

When they do, the Ponzi schemer will be unable to stem the tide of redemptions, or find new investor money to cover them. At that point, the scheme will be exposed, meeting the same inevitable end as every other fraud before it.

Before we look at the next big Ponzi scheme, it is vital that we understand what happened in the 2008 financial crisis. More Ponzi schemes were exposed then than at any other time in history.

The Financial Crisis and Ponzi Schemes

Four of the five biggest Ponzi schemes of all time were exposed in a short window during 2008-2009:

Fraudster	Fraud	Year	Amount (In Millions)
1. Bernard Madoff	Hedge Fund	2008	$65,000
2. Sergey Mavrodi	Reselling	1990	$10,000
3. Allen Stanford	Bank	2009	$8,000
4. Tom Petters	Reselling	2008	$3,700
5. Scott Rothstein	Structured Settlements	2009	$1,400

The time from 2008 to 2009 was a unique period, with economic conditions not seen since the Great Depression of the 1930s. Interest rates had dropped dramatically in years leading up to 2008, which caused investors to seek out higher returns. The higher returns came with greater risk, but as long as the markets went up, no one paid much attention.

Banks were also looking for increased profits. In the past, banks operated mostly as intermediaries, matching buyers and sellers of financial products such as options and interest rate swaps. Not only did they begin trading in these products themselves, they also invented new derivative products.

A derivative is just as it sounds: it derives its value from the underlying value of something else. It might be an option to buy stock at a locked-in price, or perhaps the ability to lock in a long-term interest rate or a bet on the future price of copper. Whatever it is, the party writing these derivative option contracts assumes the risk of potentially paying out if the event happens within the allotted time frame.

The banks wrote a lot of these contracts. Their financial analysts had crunched the numbers and calculated the odds. Their profits soared as they sold more and more of these products.

At the same time, credit was cheap and easy to get. Companies leveraged themselves with more debt to buy more equipment or expand their business. You could buy a house for little or no money down. Loan officers earned incentives to close as many mortgages as possible, so they often did not verify income or assets on the loan applications. Anyone who wanted money could get it easily, with these so-called "liar loans." Real estate speculators flipped houses and drove up housing prices further.

Financial institutions soon repackaged mortgages and commercial loans into still more products. Several loans were combined into new products, and portions of this new product sold to investors.

These products, called asset-backed commercial paper (ABCP), were short-term loans ranging from 30 to 270 days. They were backed by long-term assets such as mortgages. They allowed banks to weasel around some regulatory requirements and remove risky loans from their balance sheets. More importantly, the repackaging also disguised the high-risk subprime loans by combining them with safer loans. Just before the collapse, the ABCP market was the largest destination for investment capital, outpacing even U.S. Treasury bonds as short-term investments.

A bank would take loans with an AAA credit rating and combine them into an ABCP package with several high-risk, low credit rating loans. As long as the AAA component remained at a certain threshold percentage of the total, they could still sell the product as having an AAA credit rating. The investors in these products thought they were buying 100% AAA loans, but in fact a portion of their investment was actually subprime mortgages or so-called "liar loans."

The ABCP market unraveled in late 2007 to early 2008, and created a liquidity squeeze that ultimately started the 2008 financial crisis. As housing markets suffered a downturn, some of the ABCP holders realized that their investments held subprime mortgages, and chose not to roll over their investments. The sheer volume of these products meant that banks could not sell these products to anyone else. They had to take these loans back on their books, along with the risk that went with them.

Meanwhile, housing prices plummeted, and with little or even negative equity, people simply stopped paying their mortgages and walked away. Many of the subprime mortgages defaulted.

Everyone wanted out, but because the banks had created so much leverage, there wasn't enough money to pay back investors as the notes became due. In addition, the banks did not have enough assets to offset their increased liabilities and still meet regulatory capital requirements. The banks were effectively insolvent, and fear set in motion the biggest financial crisis since the Great Depression.

The rest of the story is a book in itself, but you get the picture. Without government intervention in most countries worldwide, the entire global banking and financial system would have collapsed. In some countries like Iceland, it did. It felt like a repeat of the

Great Depression, except this time the government took swift, albeit controversial, action.

Many countries increased deposit insurance guarantees to prevent people from withdrawing cash. Many banks worldwide were nationalized, and global governments worked in concert to prop up the global banking system.

Quick government action did not spare us pain, however. It only delayed the inevitable. Since 2008, governments have been pumping liquidity into the financial system to gradually resolve the mess we are in. In the United States, this started with TARP (Troubled Asset Relief Program) loans from the government. It progressed in the U.S. and other countries to quantitative easing (also referred to as QE1, QE2 & QE3 in the U.S.), a government monetary policy tool of last resort. The U.S. Federal Reserve bought (and is still buying) large amounts of mortgage-backed securities from the banks.

The alternative of letting all banks fail would have resulted in a much bigger catastrophe. However, the bailout does have a high price, and future generations of taxpayers will be paying for these transgressions for many decades to come.

We are left with cash-strapped governments, who as lenders of last resort bear the end result of all those subprime loans and exotic derivatives. The new danger is that we will collectively keep up our spending ways and create new asset bubbles. Like drug addicts, we have become dependent on easy credit.

The financial crisis happened despite safeguards that had been in place for decades to prevent the bank collapses and in spite of extensive government bailouts worldwide. We narrowly escaped a complete failure of the global financial system.

During the height of the 2008 financial crisis, many people lost faith in the financial system and decided to redeem investments, especially those in hedge funds or equity markets. Many investment professionals were even concerned enough to close bank accounts. This was the catalyst that brought many Ponzi schemes like Madoff's and Stanford's to ruin.

However, not everyone redeemed their investments, and some large Ponzi schemes certainly escaped detection. Depending on their so-called track record of returns and reputation, their investors might have chosen not to withdraw their money. Especially if their investments had early-redemption penalties, or if their funds were so exclusive that they were hard to get into in the first place.

The 2008 financial crisis is behind us, so why is all this important? Because we might not be out of the woods yet. The economic bounce has only bought us some time, and our governments cannot afford to inject liquidity into the economy, or keep interest rates artificially low forever. Governments have used almost every weapon in their arsenals, and they might not be strong enough to withstand the next shock wave of belt-tightening.

At some point, governments will no longer be able to issue more debt or print more money. The result will be immediately felt in the financial markets as liquidity vanishes. With less money to lend, the global economy begins to deleverage. Less capital to invest means some highly leveraged investors will need to redeem investments, including their best-performing ones. When they do, they may be in for a nasty surprise. It is here that the next big Ponzi will collapse.

History Always Repeats

What does all this have to do with the next big Ponzi? History always repeats, just never quite in the way we expect.

While there were many contributing factors to the 2008-2009 financial crisis, liquidity was the key driver. Most financial dilemmas can be cured with a change in interest rates, currencies or government intervention, providing there is adequate liquidity. Without it, there is a limit as to how many EU countries Germany can bail out, or how much debt the U.S. government can issue.

Liquidity greases the wheels and keeps them turning. Investors and borrowers may see more or less return (or cost), but they can still get what they want for a price. Like a soup, liquidity can be concentrated or diluted at will as long as everyone stays in the game. Alternatively, if liquidity dries up, our entire financial system grinds to a halt, and panic ensues.

The cure for the latest financial crisis could very well be the catalyst for the next crisis. Except the next time, there will not be any additional liquidity to inject. Timing is key. Global governments have exhausted their resources and need some breathing room. If there is another financial shock too soon, there will not be enough liquidity to repeat the process. Part two of the financial crisis will ensue, and the resulting shockwave will expose the next big Ponzi.

Can we predict the exposure of the next big Ponzi scheme? I think we can. Ponzi schemes can exist anytime and anywhere, but they proliferate—and also collapse—under certain conditions.

It is not so much that Ponzi schemes happen at a certain time, but rather that they are *discovered* at a certain time. There are certain catalysts that cause the Ponzi schemes to collapse in the first place. If we can predict these triggers, we can determine when a Ponzi scheme is likely to be exposed. To do that, we first need to look at the building blocks of Ponzi schemes and the fraudsters who start them.

Building the Ponzi

In every period leading up to the present, investors have always looked for the maximum return. We saw several billion-dollar Ponzi schemes collapse since the 2008 financial crisis, and many smaller ones. Some however, survived. These funds weathered the crisis better than Madoff, Stanford or Rothstein, but they can't continue on indefinitely.

The biggest Ponzi schemes often have the most staying power. Their sheer size means they likely have many more investors. You might assume this would increase their odds of detection, but things often work differently when there are large sums of money involved. Like Madoff's hedge fund, many of these investors will have rolled over their money in the fund for years, likely adding more as their wealth increased over the years. Having many investors lessens the possibility they will all redeem at once.

The Investors

Ponzi schemes and investments in general have grown over the last decade simply from the demographic bulge of the baby boomers. This group is more pronounced in some countries than others, an outcome of the end of the Second World War. It represents a large generational wealth transfer that was just gathering steam as the 2008 financial crisis hit.

Many baby boomers are retired or near retirement. Aside from their retirement savings, many also have inherited wealth from parents who grew up during the Great Depression, and learned how to save and put away money. Barring catastrophe, the boomers do not plan to touch or redeem any of their investments for a very long time.

People at or near retirement are the prime targets of Ponzi schemers, simply because they are at the peak of their wealth, and they are looking for a place to park their money. This factored into the last wave of Ponzi collapses, but it will become more pronounced as more baby boomers retire.

If you fit into this category, now might be a very good time to review your investments to see if there are any red flags warranting further investigation. You might be in a Ponzi scheme and not know it.

Finally, the biggest funds attract the wealthiest of investors, charities, and institutions. Madoff's investors included several billionaires and many high profile charities and foundations. Some were endowment funds, which had rules stipulating that only 5% or some similar percentage could be withdrawn. This strategy works well, because it results in predictable, small, redemptions over a very long time frame. I believe the next big Ponzi will have the same clientele.

Fertile Ground

The company running the next Ponzi is likely to originate in the United States or the United Kingdom. Both countries are top locations for hedge funds globally. Seventy- five percent of European hedge funds are domiciled in London.

The management will likely be headquartered in London or New York. Since we are looking for a sham, the focus here is on the management's location, and not that of the funds themselves. However, the complex or foreign aspects of Ponzi schemes often mean that the so-called funds or underlying investments might be based offshore, possibly in the Caribbean, or a secretive tax haven. Many wealthy people have established trusts and keep their investments offshore to avoid taxes, like Stanford's fraud in Antigua.

While Florida is a hotspot, frauds there are typically on a smaller scale, with Rothstein being a notable exception.

Despite Europe's large capital markets, I think the next big Ponzi scheme is less likely to occur there.

There is a difference in the social and political climate in European countries in general in comparison with the free enterprise focus of the United States. Many European states have generous pensions, which leaves less investing (and fewer investment decisions) in the hands of individuals. In the U.S., the system is less state supported and more up to the individual. Hence, a rich landscape to troll for victims.

Since four of the top five Ponzi schemes discovered occurred in the United States, there is a high probability we will find the next one there also. As it will be the largest Ponzi exposed to date, it will be long established and will likely be comprised of many wealthy investors. It will likely be located where investment capital and old money congregate, such as New York. New York also happens to be one of the most populous states, along with California, Texas and Florida, so there is greater likelihood of fraud occurring in any of these states.

Timing

There are enough common threads to make some bold assumptions on the timing of this Ponzi collapse. Interest rates are still at historical lows, and government bailouts and market interventions have continued the era of easy money to avoid total financial collapse. This approach allows financial markets, and investor confidence, to recover. However, it also encourages a new cycle of the same behavior that caused the financial crisis in the first place. It increases the likelihood and magnitude of another financial crisis, especially in the next few years, as speculators and others take on more risk in search of higher returns.

Given that the U.S. Federal Reserve has indicated that it intends to stop quantitative easing as early as 2014, we can expect liquidity to dry up shortly thereafter. Although the central bank's actions may be gradual, the boomerang effect throughout the financial markets may be more sudden. When banks have fewer funds available from the Federal Reserve, they will make fewer loans, resulting in fewer investments made. Markets tend to factor in news in advance of actual events. For this reason, I believe a significant market contraction will occur, the timing dependent on when QE actually does end.

The Year

The current government intervention will continue to keep everything running for one to two years after the quantitative easing monetary policy ends. With no new debt, credit and liquidity will sharply contract. As it will take some time for this to be felt, I predict this financial contraction will begin to have acute repercussions in 2016.

Coincidentally, 2016 also happens to be a U.S. election year. Election years are usually positive for financial markets. However, this time it will be different. No matter what political party is elected to the highest office, there will be a new president, since Obama will have served his second term. Add the uncertainty of a new president with no more tools to intervene in the market to manage liquidity, and you have a recipe for another financial crisis. There is no room for error.

The Month

If past history is an indication, we can also pinpoint the time of year in which the next Ponzi scheme collapse will occur. Most Ponzi schemes are exposed in the last quarter of any given year, specifically between September and December.

Why are they concentrated in the latter half of the year?

Investors often redeem their winning investments to offset tax losses in the same year to avoid paying tax. They tend to execute on this near the end of the calendar year, such as October to December.

A second reason is the funds themselves. Some Ponzi schemes are self-described as hedge funds and are thus required to report their holdings on at least an annual basis. Most of these funds have a December 31 year end.

The fund manager must report all the holdings—usually in an annual report or quarterly report. Not only is it a huge undertaking to falsify numerous financial records, but they have to be fabricated well enough to pass the scrutiny of an external auditor, and/or regulatory authorities. As the date approaches, certain investment managers might decide to stop the sham, as they might be unable to keep juggling all the balls in the air.

Most major market corrections in recent years have happened between September and December. While the correction might be abrupt and steep, some investors might take their time in deciding whether they should withdraw their money or not. Others will act immediately, and their actions will reinforce another selloff and steep market decline. At this point, more people might redeem their investments, and the Ponzi operator will become squeezed for cash. The fraudster can no longer pay the clamoring investors banging on his door. This usually happens several months after the initial market crash, at the point where the fraudster can no longer dream up excuses to persuade the investor to keep money in the scheme. The scam fund can't pay the monthly interest payments either, so after a couple of missed payments chances are at least one investor will report his suspicions to authorities, realizing in hindsight that he's been duped.

We can also be reasonably certain of when the Ponzi scheme collapse will *not* happen. Generally, the market is quieter in the summer, when people take vacation time. The old saying "Sell in May and go away" stems from the fact that there is less trading activity and less volatility in the summer months from May to September.

This trading pattern is not as random as it seems. Fall is a time of fresh starts and increased activity after summer. That includes investment people returning from vacation, investors re-evaluating their portfolios, and an increased volume of economic news. It is only natural that people are more likely to absorb, evaluate, and act on bad news at this time.

The Ponzi scheme is likely to be revealed in November, after a month of high volatility trading in

October, and as investors consider year-end tax-loss selling or portfolio rebalancing.

The Day—Monday

The day of the week might be the easiest of all to predict for the revelation of the Ponzi scheme. Consider the case of fraud impacting a publicly traded company. There are strict regulations governing the release of information. Any news affecting trading activity must be released when the markets are closed. News releases, especially negative ones, tend to happen on the weekend. The hope is that there is time for any bad news to be overshadowed by something else, or else be disseminated and accepted before the start of business on Monday.

In the case of a Ponzi scheme, authorities will take several actions in advance of an announcement. They want to ensure they have everything in order and not tip off the fraudster in advance. In many cases, they will shut down the operation on a Friday afternoon, with the intent of announcing charges early Monday morning.

They will be prepared with search warrants for the suspect's premises, and freeze assets such as bank accounts. To substantiate the charges to the greatest extent possible, they will need time to examine the books and records. The first opportunity to review records in any great detail is at this point, so they will use the weekend to search through records as much as possible to determine potential charges. A team of forensic accountants and fraud experts will comb through the books and freeze any connected assets at other institutions or those in other jurisdictions. By following the money trail, they are likely to uncover previously unknown assets. All asset discovery increases the chance of recovery.

Now that we have determined that this Ponzi will be publicly exposed in the U.S. on a Monday in November, 2016, which Monday will it be?

November 7 can be dismissed as it is the day before Election Day, and November 21 and 28 are too close to Thanksgiving. By process of elimination, that leaves Monday, November 14 as the most probable day of all.

The Ultimate Ponzi—Who, What, When and Where

Given that we can predict the environment and the date, what will this Ponzi scheme look like? It will be at least on the scale of Madoff's, but almost certainly bigger, since it already weathered the 2008 financial crisis. Like Madoff's fund, it has likely operated for decades. If past history is at all a predictor of the future, it will be represented as either a straight hedge fund, like Madoff's, or some sort of broker type arrangement where the investor gets a cut off the top, like Rothstein's structured settlements or Shapiro's or Mavrodi's reselling of groceries or electronics respectively. The most likely scenario is something outside the regulatory umbrella of the SEC, like Rothstein's structured settlements scam.

Secrets Uncovered

Like many of the Ponzi schemes in this book, there will probably have been suspicions around this yet-undiscovered Ponzi scheme long before it is exposed. Both Madoff and Stanford's purported returns were reverse-engineered by other investment professionals who were unable to replicate the reported performance numbers. They even reported their suspicions to the SEC, but these concerns were not immediately acted upon.

Of the top five Ponzi schemes in this book, none were directly uncovered by regulatory authorities. Bernard Madoff turned himself in. Whistleblower complaints about him several years earlier had been ignored. Sergey Mavrodi's tax evasion investigation triggered the discovery of his fraud.

Allen Stanford's fraud was reverse-engineered by an analyst, but no immediate action was taken. Tom Petters' crime was only discovered when his longtime employee turned evidence over to authorities, and Scott Rothstein's scam was discovered during his high-drama flight to Morocco with millions in tow.

The Ponzi schemes were all revealed by someone other than the authorities, just at the point when they were about to collapse.

Can We Expose it Before Collapse?

Given that Madoff's $65 billion fraud wasn't big enough to withstand the 2008 financial crisis, and assuming this one did, it is probably at least a $100 billion dollar scheme.

Assuming this is true, how can we find such a scheme before it implodes? One way might be to look at where the ultra-rich invest. These people are specifically targeted by scammers, not only for their wealth, but also because they tend to be secretive. This secrecy works in the Ponzi schemer's favor.

Perhaps an easier way is to look for the largest investments held by charitable organizations or endowment funds. The Ponzi schemer is likely to have convinced them to invest more after early successes, hence it will be among their largest holdings. A Ponzi scheme with endowment funds that only redeem 5% a year, as in Madoff's fraud, means that the Ponzi schemer will not have to deal with large redemptions, and the money stays invested for decades.

This is the most likely scenario, but the scheme could include many types of investors, and you could be one of them. Compare each of your investments against the Ponzi checklist at the end of the book. Do they pass the test? Like an incestuous relationship or an illicit affair, a con artist's success depends on the gullibility of the people he or she victimizes.

After you have reviewed your investments against the checklist, note any that meet the checklist criteria. Now shift your attention to the head honcho. What can you find out about him? Does he lead an extravagant lifestyle, or has he donated millions to many charitable organizations? This in itself does not indicate dishonesty, however most or all Ponzi schemers will lead very extravagant lifestyles. Overt displays of wealth and over the top altruism can indicate ill-gotten gains and that something is amiss.

Before and after the big one is uncovered, there will be many other Ponzi schemes uncovered. However, the next big one will elicit a collective gasp from all of us.

The Next Big Ponzi—A Prediction

The Likely Culprit

Can we pinpoint the fraudster to an even greater degree? Based on the profiles earlier in this book, we can likely determine character traits, though some of these might only be obvious in hindsight. Most notable is a lack of conscience or remorse, and an outsized ego and sense of entitlement.

Besides psychological and personality traits, can we more specifically profile such a person? To some extent, we can look at past frauds for clues to future ones.

Almost all of the frauds in this book were committed by men older than forty. This also bears true for frauds in general, not just Ponzi schemes. Statistically, men are not only more likely to commit fraud but tend to commit significantly larger frauds than women.

Are men more dishonest than women? Do they have a sudden propensity to steal once they hit forty? This would be too simplistic an explanation, but there seems to be some basis to the statistics.

Consider men and women's historical roles in society and the workplace. Men have outnumbered women in the workplace until the last few decades. Even today, men still vastly outnumber women in positions of authority: positions with decision-making power or access to large sums of capital. The investment sector in particular is dominated by men. The same inequality holds true in white-collar crime, since you need the opportunity to commit the crime in the first place.

This perception is changing, since women now roughly equal men in the fields of finance, law, accounting, and other professions. Yet they still occupy a disproportionate number of lower rungs on the corporate ladder, and fewer work at the top. Until this demographic changes, it is highly probable that the next big Ponzi schemer will be a man.

Assuming this is true—why not a man in his twenties? Simply because most fraud starts out small. No one starts out with a billion dollar fraud. A fraudster starts with smaller frauds, and as he finds success, he increases the scope and the size of his fraud over time. He needs time to build his contacts too—from those who refer investors to the investors themselves who repeatedly roll over their investments or bring in their friends.

It takes decades to build a multi-billion dollar fraud. Once a scammer begins to cheat on a large scale, the Ponzi scheme will mushroom as he ensnares more and more victims. Illegal activities take time to reach a critical mass, probably at least several decades.

Based on the other fraudsters we have examined, our scammer will also likely be a respected high-profile member of society. He probably makes large charitable donations, and sits on the board of one or more high-profile non-profit organizations. He will use more sophisticated technology than the fraudsters we have seen to date, and this factor might be partly why he emerged unscathed from the 2008 financial crisis.

Finally, he will appear to be ultra-wealthy with plenty of expensive toys.

The Prediction

There you have it. Odds are that the biggest Ponzi

scheme of all time will be a $100+ billion fraud exposed on Monday, November 14, 2016 in New York. The fraud will be a New York hedge fund employing a type of structured settlement strategy like Scott Rothstein's fraud. The scheme will be exposed by a rival hedge fund while trying to reverse-engineer the Ponzi scheme's stellar returns.

Our Ponzi schemer will be a highly respected man in his fifties, a lawyer or an accountant. Oh, and he'll probably drive a Bentley.

APPENDIX

USEFUL RESOURCES

The next time you are tempted by a fantastic investment opportunity, evaluate it against the Ponzi checklist below. If you check off even one of the items listed below, think twice about investing.

This checklist also holds true for any investment. Never hand over your money without first comparing your potential investment against this list.

Ponzi Checklist
1. Unusually High Returns
2. Constant Returns over Long Periods
3. Significant Returns over short period of time
4. Time-limited or Sense of Urgency
5. Unregistered Investments
6. No Prospectus
7. Unlicensed Sellers
8. Secretive or Complex Strategies
9. Foreign-based
10. Difficulty Getting Payment
11. Exclusivity
12. Incentives to Reinvestment
13. Difficulty Reaching Seller
14. Unqualified or inexperienced employees

Investor Protection and Other Resources

There is a wealth of investor protection and fraud awareness information on the Internet. Below are just a few of the government agencies and nonprofit organizations who provide fraud tips, alerts and interesting case histories.

United States
U.S. Securities and Exchange Commission
www.sec.gov
Check the investor tools section
Financial Industry Regulatory Authority
www.finra.org
www.saveandinvest.org/fraudcenter/
Financial Fraud Enforcement Task Force
www.stopfraud.gov
Federal Bureau of Investigation
www.fbi.gov
See Scams and Safety tab

North American Securities Administrators Association
www.nasaa.org
See the Top Investors Threats section
Association of Certified Fraud Examiners
www.acfe.com
See the Fraud Resources section

Canada
B.C. Securities Commission
www.befraudaware.ca
www.investright.org

Ontario Securities Commission
www.osc.gov.on.ca/en/investors

The Canadian Foundation for Advancement of
Investor Rights
www.faircanada.ca
See Investor Resources section
Canadian Securities Administrators
www.securities-administrators.ca

RCMP
www.rcmp-grc.gc.ca/scams-fraudes/inv-fra-eng.htm
Information on investment and securities fraud

Association of Certified Forensic Investigators
of Canada
www.acfi.ca

AUTHOR'S NOTE

I hope you have enjoyed reading *Anatomy of a Ponzi*. While Ponzi schemes and fraud in general fascinate me, it saddens me to hear of people being duped time and again with the same old trickery. It is truly amazing how much fraud corrupts and permeates our society. Equally surprising is how easy it is to spot, as long as you know what to look for.

Remember—if you do spot something suspicious, use the resources in this book to validate your suspicions. Above all, please report the crime, so that others might be spared financial misery.

I also write fraud thrillers. *Exit Strategy* and *Game Theory are the first two books in the Katerina Carter*

Fraud Thriller Series, and more books in the series are under development. Read the first chapter of *Exit* Strategy at the end of this book or find out more at http://www.colleencross.com/

Colleen Cross

EXIT STRATEGY

A KATERINA CARTER FRAUD THRILLER

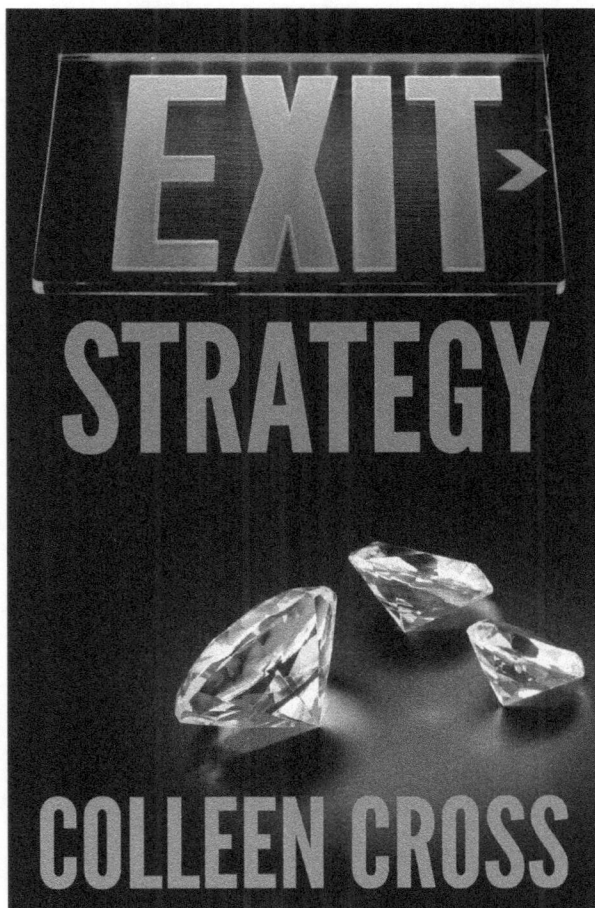

FIRST CHAPTER PREVIEW

CHAPTER 1

BUENOS AIRES, ARGENTINA

THE BEDROOM LIGHT FLASHED ON and Clara's world exploded. Three men in *masques luchadores* burst into the room and surrounded the bed like a tag team in a wrestling ring. She turned her head to look at Vicente, but saw only her husband's back.

Carnaval dance troupes paraded in the street below, all Buenos Aires oblivious to the theatre unfolding in her bedroom. Sounds of snare drums and cymbals drifted upwards as *murga porteños* beat out the final notes of the *Despidida*, the exit song.

The stocky one charged Vicente with a baseball bat, driving it down across his legs with a thud. Clara shuddered as the mattress imploded from the impact. Vicente grunted but remained still. A million images raced through her head—her mother, her father's cronies, his competitors. All those disappearances would have started like this.

Turn around.

Vicente tensed beside her. He slid his hand towards hers and clasped it under the bed sheet without looking at her. She squeezed it back as she fought to calm her racing thoughts. Their detailed plans hadn't included getting caught.

Then the man turned to Clara. He wore a garish green mask with thick red borders around his eyes and mouth. His eyes bored into hers, challenging her. She clutched at the mulberry silk coverlet with her exposed hand, pulling it upwards. The fabric reverberated with every beat of her racing heart.

The diamonds. Her father knew about the plan.

"Name your price. I'll pay you." Her words came in a whisper.

They'd delayed their escape by two days, waiting for payment on the last diamond shipment. Vicente objected, insisting a year of preparation shouldn't be undone in one day. But Clara needed to wrench every last peso from her father, to ruin him, to make him pay. She would prove she could outsmart him, just like she had for the last two years. Now their escape was in jeopardy. How had he found out?

"You can't buy me, Clara." Rodriguez didn't bother disguising his voice, either too stupid or too cocky to worry about it.

"Why not? My father did. How much do you want?" She kept her voice even as bile rose in her throat. Her father had sent Rodriguez on purpose, knowing she despised him.

Vicente squeezed her hand; now it was damp with sweat. The two other men remained at the foot of the bed, AK47s trained on them both.

"It's not money I want." He pulled off the mask, the overhead light glinting off his gold tooth. "You can still choose me. At least I've got a future."

The tall, rangy one in the Wolfman mask laughed and shifted his gun.

Bastard. She wasn't a prize to be married off. And Rodriguez might think he was in her father's inner circle, but Clara knew better. It could just as easily be Rodriguez in the gun sights instead. Like a tank of lobsters, sooner or later it would be his turn.

Vicente shot up in bed. "Leave her out of this."

Clara pulled at Vicente's forearm. Even she knew not to anger Rodriguez. He wasn't known as the executioner for nothing.

"Shut up." Rodriguez shoved Vicente back down on the bed with the rifle butt.

"Call my father. It's a misunderstanding." She could explain away the diamonds and convince him of even greater profits. Her idea of trading guns and munitions for blood diamonds had been a cash cow for the organization, but her father couldn't even spare a thank you. So Clara and Vicente had helped themselves to a cut off the top. They deserved it.

"Too late. He's out of the country. Out of contact."

"Liar. Call him, Rodriguez. I'm ordering you to—right now!"

Rodriguez was little more than a glorified thug, having risen through the ranks of her father's organization by being willing to do anything, kill anyone. How could he know her father planned to transfer the day-to-day running of the cartel to Vicente. Or so he said. They had dined with him at Resto, her favorite restaurant, just hours ago. Was her father dispatching his thugs while they ate? No, he likely choreographed both the dinner and punishment days before, waiting for the ultimate moment of revenge. The irony would have thrilled him.

"I don't take instruction from spoiled brats."

"Call him right now!" Clara almost sat up, forgetting her nakedness under the sheets.

"No. It's time I got a little of what I want." Rodriguez moved slowly over to her side of the bed. Wolfman and el Diablo remained by the wall, guns trained at their heads. Vicente shifted on the mattress beside her and squeezed her hand under the sheets.

Clara tried a softer tone.

"Please—I need to talk to my father."

"Talk to him at Vicente's funeral." Rodriguez turned and strode back towards the other men. He motioned to them with a flick of the wrist and disappeared into the bathroom.

The men lowered their guns slightly as first one then the other scanned the covers, starting at her feet and moving up slowly to meet her stare. She didn't need to see their faces to know what they were thinking. She felt it.

Clara shuddered as she tugged on the coverlet. Wolfman laughed at her and moved closer. Obviously one of her father's henchmen, but one she didn't recognize.

He hooked the barrel of his gun under the comforter edge and pulled it off. Not once did he take his eyes off hers. Clara shivered but didn't dare move.

Vicente tensed beside her.

The sheer curtains fluttered as a soft breeze blew into the bedroom. The revelers had gone and it was almost dawn. Already she could hear the faint sounds of traffic on nearby Avenida Libertador as more law abiding *porteños* began their predictable workdays. What she wouldn't give for such tedium right now.

"Get the door," Wolfman said to el Diablo, motioning towards the hallway while keeping his eyes locked on hers.

Then he moved closer, still pointing the gun at her head and reeking of stale cigars. He sat down on the side of the bed, blocking the open window. Suddenly the room felt stifling and claustrophobic.

Rodriguez emerged from the bathroom and the man stood up quickly.

"Not now," Rodriguez said as he motioned Wolfman back against the wall. He turned back to Vicente. "Get up, asshole."

Vicente let go of her hand. She felt it slide upwards towards the pillow where he kept his gun.

"None of that shit. Turn around. Hands out or I'll cut them off."

Rodriguez relished his command over Vicente.

Vicente did as he was told.

"Get up. Slowly."

Still with his back to her—she couldn't see his eyes.

"Give me a minute."

"I'm not giving you anything, moron. Do it now."

Vicente stumbled to his feet, nude. He held his arms up in surrender.

"In the bathroom. Now." Rodriguez shoved him with the gun barrel hard against Vicente's back, pushing him forward.

"No!" Clara grabbed her water glass from the bedside table and hurled it at Rodriguez. It missed and shattered against the wall.

Vicente turned to steal a look at her.

"Mi amor, nuestro sueño. Nunca olvides."

He stumbled as Rodriguez rammed the rifle butt into his back.

His face was etched in her mind when the shooting started.

Our dream. Never forget.

Never.

Her last thought was drowned out by the staccato of gunfire.

Then everything went black.

ABOUT THE AUTHOR

Colleen Cross is the author of *Anatomy of a Ponzi, Scams Past and Present, as well as* The Katerina Carter Fraud Thriller Series. She is also an accountant. She lives near Vancouver, Canada.

To keep up to date with Colleen's latest books and events, please visit her website at http://www.colleencross.com.

You can also become a fan on Goodreads, Facebook, or follow her on Twitter: @colleenxcross

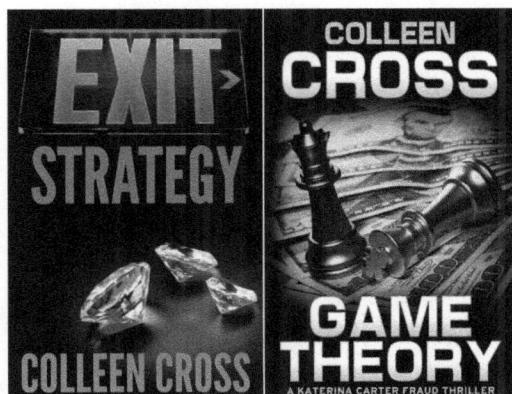

www.ingramcontent.com/pod-product-compliance
Lightning Source LLC
Chambersburg PA
CBHW020830210326
41598CB00019B/1861